The Divorce Handbook

THE DIVORCE HANDBOOK

Your Basic Guide to Divorce

Updated Edition

James T. Friedman

RANDOM HOUSE
New York

Library of Congress Cataloging in Publication Data

Friedman, James T., 1936–
    The divorce handbook.

    Bibliography: p.
        1. Divorce—United States—Handbooks, manuals, etc.
2. Divorce—Law and legislation—United States—Handbooks,
manuals, etc.   I. Title.
HQ834.F74   1984   346.7301'66   83–43211
ISBN 0-394-72327-9 (pbk.)   347.306166

Manufactured in the United States of America
9 8 7 6

**To Sol R. Friedman,
divorce lawyer**

Acknowledgment

The author gratefully acknowledges the artful nagging, tireless proofreading, and valuable advice of Errol Zavett, Phyllis Rusano, Patricia Rader, Barbara Czrnekovic, and Carolyn Friedman. Without them this book would have been possible, but not probable.

Alphabetical Summary of Check Lists, Guides, Sample Schedules and Worksheets

CONTENTS

VI. Child Support and Visitation   33

VII. Financial Hide-and-Seek with Your Spouse   40

XIV. The Trial 110

The Divorce Handbook

Chapter I

WHO NEEDS
THIS HANDBOOK:
How to Use it

1. Who needs this handbook?

Every person who is thinking about a divorce or is in the process of getting one.

The book is designed as a practical guide to take you chronologically through the various stages from the first time the subject crosses your mind to the final decree and closing your file. No one person experiences *all* of the steps included in this book, because every divorce differs as to the areas of disagreement and extent to which certain issues may be contested in court. The question-answer format allows you to read only what concerns you at the moment. Reading from cover to cover will give you a perspective on the entire divorcing process.

2. Why do I need this handbook?

A major part of the emotional stress of divorce is being involved in something you don't understand. Divorce unleashes fears of material loss as well as feelings of abandonment and guilt, thus clouding your ability to think clearly about financial settlements, personal needs, and the needs of your children.

Divorce places you at the mercy of a system which has its own language and procedures and which seems to move people about like pawns from one courtroom to the next.

For example, if you have experienced any of the following predicaments, you need this workbook.

- One day you want a divorce and the next day you want a marriage counselor.
- You don't want a divorce but your spouse just filed for one— or has mentioned the possibility.
- You have just come from your first appointment with a lawyer and he used a number of words you didn't understand but didn't ask him to explain.
- Your spouse is jeopardizing your job with phone calls to your employer and/or lies to your friends and co-workers.
- Your spouse has missed his temporary support payment for the tenth time.
- Every time you call your lawyer you forget two points of the five that you wanted to cover—because he sounds in a hurry.
- Your divorce seems to be standing still—and you're standing in quicksand.
- With inflation you're bleeding from support payments. Can they be modified?
- Court continuances are ruining your schedule. Doesn't anybody else work?
- Your lawyer is in court or in conference every time you call.
- You never know when you'll see your children. They seem brainwashed against you.
- The silver and the piano are missing.
- You have agreed to too large a support payment, and can't manage financially.
- You feel helpless and your life seems out of control.

3. How can a lawyer use this handbook?

By using it with you as a guide at various stages of your case. If, for example, he suggests you review the Hidden Asset Check List on page 49, you may help uncover assets that never would have been discovered otherwise. Application of your factual situation to the sample trial outlines will enable you and your lawyer to save hours in trial preparation, and you'll both be thinking on the same wavelength. A secretary or paralegal can also use the outlines and check lists to assist you in the preparation of your case at less expense. Lack of communication is the greatest single problem between busy divorce lawyers and emotional clients. This handbook provides you with a common source of communication and should be the basis for your organization and preparation at every stage of negotiation or litigation.

4. How can this handbook help me?

It guides you through the divorcing process step by step and provides perspective—an overview of where you are now and should expect to be later. This handbook puts you in charge of your life at this difficult time.

- It identifies important information relevant to your case.
- It also tells you where, when, and how to find that information.
- It organizes and stores the information in one readily available place.
- It reduces your insecurity and frustration by involving you in the process and showing that you are not alone.
- It helps you select a lawyer and deal with him or her effectively.
- It enables the lawyer to give better answers because you will ask better questions.
- It provides resource information for particular problems through an extensive bibliography.
- It provides a glossary of legal terms common to divorce.
- It's your security blanket—and it covers everything you'll need to know about the divorcing process.
- It puts you in the habit of asking questions. Even if you think you know the answer—ask!

5. Why can't I let my lawyer do it all?

Because he probably won't. And can't.

For one thing, he is too busy to answer every question at length, and for another, you probably won't know the right ones to ask. Your frustration will grow in direct proportion to the court orders, continuances, judgments, and situations you do not understand or know how to handle.

Furthermore, your lawyer should not do it all. It is your responsibility to find and organize the necessary records and documents. Few people—or lawyers—can afford to pay an accountant or other professional just to gather information and put it in usable form for the case.

You should not be a passive participant in your own divorce. You, the client, have a vital role to play in the divorcing process.

6. Why can't my recently divorced friends advise me?

Every divorce case and set of circumstances are different. Your friend may have four more children than you do, or none. She may have a trust fund or he may like the vegetarian life. They may have living parents with a guesthouse, a supermarket in the family, or a brother-in-law who is a plumber. Remember, each divorce is unique—like the marriage that preceded it.

However, you can learn from your friends' mistakes. Do get practical information regarding their settlement agreements— copies of the actual agreements if possible. Ask them: What would you do differently? Would you use the same lawyer?

CAUTION: Remember, friends' priorities are not necessarily the same as yours. They may also have conflicting loyalties to you and your spouse.

7. What does this handbook include?

Basic information on divorce in a question-and-answer format.
Practical and do-able suggestions.
Worksheets.
Check lists.
Glossary—so you understand the language.
Bibliography.
Questions you need to ask yourself and your lawyer.
Answers you have to have!

8. What does this handbook leave out?

Detailed tables presenting the laws of each state on grounds, property, alimony, and maintenance, child support and child custody, residency requirements, etc. These laws change regularly and require legal interpretation to be fully understood. An experienced local lawyer is the best source for this information.

9. How do I use this handbook?

You can read from cover to cover to get a detailed overview of a contested divorce from beginning to end.

You can look over the Contents when you have a particular problem. Just read the answers or use the check lists, guides, and schedules, starting at page 20, that concern you at the moment. Determine what information and documents you need. File documents you already have in an envelope. Cross them off the check list and begin searching for missing documents or other information important to your case. Contact the people who can give you the information or documents you still need. The Internal Revenue Service, your bank, your broker (stock, real estate, and insurance), or your doctor may provide valuable information. Former neighbors or friends might make good witnesses if a trial becomes necessary.

Find their present addresses and phone numbers. Mark them down on your Witness List.

In any event, take this book to an early appointment with your lawyer to discuss what may be relevant to your case. Have him review check lists with you and get specific directions as to what he will need and when.

CAUTION: If your case is contested, keep your records where your spouse won't find them. If no safe place is available in your home, keep them with a trusted friend. There is no point in letting the other side know your strategy or how much information you have gathered or lack. Also, it may be a good idea to photocopy and replace documents when you don't need the originals. If your spouse alters or "misplaces" the documents later on, you will have a valuable record and a possible basis for discrediting him or her, which the court calls impeachment.

Chapter II

DIVORCE AT YOUR DOORSTEP

10. When does the divorce begin?

When you or your spouse first seriously think about ending the marriage. Every married person thinks about divorce or separation from time to time. When these thoughts linger *after* the anger or frustration has passed, they are a signal to *do something* because your marriage is breaking down. When the "I want out" thoughts dominate the desire to work things out and you start considering the practical aspects of separation or divorce (change of residence, living expenses, effect on the children)—the divorcing process has begun.

Once begun, the process does not have to end in a divorce. It is the willingness to do something positive as soon as you recognize the process beginning that gives you the best chance of reconciliation.

11. Should I stay married for the sake of the children?

Probably not, if they are the *only thing* keeping you together. The coldness or hostility displayed by you and your spouse is bad for the children and may even interfere later with their own marriages. In reality, though, people rarely remain together just for the sake of the children. Most of the time there are other factors at play, sometimes unconscious ones.

In fact, other gratifications from a relationship can keep an estranged couple together, even though their marriage is dead. Arrangements sometimes develop between married couples where they only share the household because it is economically or socially convenient. They create their own separate lives within the home, without interfering with or substantially annoying the other. Parties living in a state of truce for many years will often divorce after the youngest child is out on his own.

If no such gratifications exist for you, then deal with your marital problem realistically. Don't just ignore the deterioration of your marriage or mope around about it—solve it, adjust to it, or separate. Too much self-sacrifice can be intolerable to your children as well as your spouse.

12. I don't want a divorce. Should I fight it?

Yes, at least to the point where you are sure the marriage cannot be saved. At that point your resistance should be geared only to what's necessary to obtain a fair settlement. Not wanting the divorce is usually a key leverage factor because the party anxious for the divorce will usually *buy* his or her way out—offer inducements to change your mind. Let them induce.

On the other hand, if you overplay your leverage with unreasonable demands or fight the divorce out of vindictiveness or self-righteousness, the result is likely to be economic and emotional devastation for your entire family. Fight only where there's a positive result to be achieved.

13. I want a divorce. Can't I just leave?

Yes, you can, but talk to a lawer *before* you make this crucial decision. In a potentially litigated divorce a number of strategic considerations argue against a spouse's leaving the marital home. For example, if a wife or a husband seeking custody of the children leaves home without the children, he or she may be at a substantial disadvantage when the actual custody proceedings begin.

A physical separation may also have a lot to do with the timing of the divorce. If, for example, your spouse wants you out of the house but is reluctant to agree to a divorce, it may be a strategic error to move. Once you're gone, your spouse's desire to separate has been satisfied and there is no need to speed along the divorce proceedings. Your spouse can then obtain repeated continuances of court proceedings or make arbitrary settlement demands in order to delay resolution of your case. The more this delay frustrates you, the more of a leverage factor it becomes. You will ultimately pay more or receive less in order to settle the case. *Refusing* to leave the house when your spouse wants you out reverses the leverage. The greater the "want," the greater the leverage that can be employed to achieve concessions in other areas of negotiation.

If you believe there is a genuine physical danger to you, your children, or your spouse, get out now regardless of the legal consequences. You are concerned with money, property, and the like, but it is hard to enjoy any of them in a body cast or a pine box.

CAUTION: Fault states are those in which marital misconduct must be proved before divorce can be granted. Illinois and South Dakota are the only fault states. In these states leaving the marital home can be construed as desertion if the statutory period of separation is met. Only when the departing spouse can prove good cause for leaving can the separation be construed as "constructive" desertion and provide grounds for divorce for the departing spouse.

14. Can a separation save the marriage?

Sometimes, yes. Physical proximity can be a great source of antagonism for couples considering divorce. A change in the status quo is often the first step to saving the marriage. The new perspective gained by separation may help you discover the cause of your dissatisfaction. The actual experience of separation provides a testing period that can alter perceptions of divorce as a solution. The party who is pushing for a divorce on the mistaken belief that physical separation will resolve his or her unhappiness often finds that the contrary is true. Separation then may provide new insight into the cause of unhappiness or the advisability of resuming the marital relationship.

15. If I leave the house voluntarily, can I get back in?

The longer you are gone, the more difficult reentry is likely to be if your spouse opposes it. Even if you have a written agreement that says your leaving will not prejudice your right to return, courts are sometimes reluctant to enforce these agreements if the separation has been a long one. Very often a spouse who is sincerely interested in saving the marriage will agree to leave in order to give the other spouse an opportunity to reconsider. However, by making such an arrangement, the departing spouse takes a very real chance that no reentry will be possible.

CAUTION: See a lawyer before leaving.

10

16. How do I get or give financial support during a separation if no court action is pending?

Support is obtained by agreement with the other spouse or by taking possession of marital assets and using them to satisfy your support needs. A joint bank account, for example, is the most liquid asset for satisfying immediate needs, unless you have cash in a cookie jar or safe-deposit box. If liquid assets aren't available, some women out of desperation have sold their jewelry or household furniture to put food on the table. In most cases, unless income is clearly inadequate, relief can be obtained from the court before it's necessary to sell personal property. If your spouse can contribute to support but won't, get into court as soon as possible to avoid dissipation of family assets. A nonsupporter will most likely be hiding assets as well.

17. Do voluntary payments set a precedent?

Yes, very often they do in terms of amount. If a supporting spouse has voluntarily been paying $200 a week for an extended period, it may be difficult to convince the court at a later time of an inability to pay that amount, unless there is proof of a substantial change in financial circumstances.

CAUTION: If the supporting spouse is eager to bring the divorce to a conclusion, he or she may inadvertently delay final settlement by meeting *all* the financial needs of the other spouse who is content to remain in a separated and supported condition. A delicate balance must be maintained in arriving at a support figure prior to formal divorce proceedings. If this figure is unreasonably low, it provokes the animosity of the other spouse and escalates the contested aspect of the proceedings. If it is too high, it sets a precedent which raises the level of expectation of the recipient spouse, who will settle for nothing less. A temporary support figure that is too high or too low becomes a leverage factor that will speed up settlement of the case only if the spouse who pays less or receives more than he or she should is also the one who is anxious to settle. That spouse can voluntarily modify the support as an inducement to a permanent settlement.

18. Can I date during the separation?

Casual dating will not legally affect the granting of the divorce, the award of custody and support, or the division of property. However, if your dating involves considerable time spent away from the children or staying out overnight, the dating may take on the aspect of moral misconduct and can affect some of the issues in your case.

The attitude of your spouse is also important. If dating makes your spouse jealous, the vindictive reaction will certainly slow down the resolution of your case. If frequent dating of the same person indicates an intention of early remarriage, you are providing your spouse with a useful leverage factor to reduce your share of the settlement. It is best to consult with your attorney before you get involved in any regular or serious dating.

CAUTION: Your spouse may encourage you to date in order to point an accusing finger at you during divorce proceedings. Be careful and discreet.

19. What about sexual relations with my spouse once a divorce is likely?

There is no definitive answer to this question. In states that recognize condonation as a defense to divorce, you may lose your grounds by continued marital relations. You may also delude yourself or your spouse into a false hope of reconciliation through continued sexual relations. Your good sense and your attorney's advice will be required to make this important decision.

20. How do I deal with physical violence?

Call the police or sheriff's office in your community. Although police are reluctant to involve themselves in domestic disputes, they necessarily do so on a regular basis. Criminal charges for assault and battery or child abuse should be brought where appropriate. Your spouse has no more right to physically abuse you or your child than a stranger would have.

A peace bond may be sought from the criminal court with the assistance of your local police as a substitute for a divorce court injunction. If you can prove that your spouse has been physically abusive, the court will require the posting of a cash bond which will be forfeited if the abuse is repeated. The threat of financial loss can sometimes be an effective psychological deterrent for a spouse inclined to physical violence. If it is regularly necessary to seek police aid to quell domestic disturbances, you need psychiatric intervention, or separation, or divorce, or all three.

21. It looks like divorce. How do I protect myself?

See a lawyer as soon as possible. You don't have to hire one, but you must learn what your rights and obligations are in regard to your spouse and your family. There are many books and pamphlets on divorce and separation that discuss property rights, support rights, and custody rights. (Some are listed in the

Bibliography at the end of this book.) But *no* book or pamphlet or person untrained in the law *as it applies in your community* can advise you adequately. The written law of your state (statutes) interpreted by your appellate courts, as well as the application of those laws in your local courts, will determine your rights and responsibilities.

CAUTION: This book does not list or discuss particular state divorce laws because no two states are the same, and those laws change every day. A local lawyer can best advise on your local law and appropriate strategy. We emphasize procedures and techniques in the divorcing process that will enable you to ask your attorney better questions and understand the answers better too.

22. How should I deal with my spouse during the divorce?

Divorce tends to bring out the worst in people. Self-interest apparently justifies deceptions and outright lies which would be intolerable to nice people in ordinary times. Self-protection requires a new set of guidelines for dealing with your legal adversary:

1. If love is gone, substitute politeness.
2. Be skeptical. Half of what is said is meant to deceive you. The other half is self-deception.
3. Breast your cards. Don't let your spouse know how much you know.
4. Walk away from arguments or conflict.
5. Expect your spouse to resent your lawyer and to attempt to undermine his influence.
6. Don't enter into private negotiations without your lawyer's knowledge and advice.
7. Don't make agreements or sign anything without talking to your lawyer first.
8. When in doubt, believe your lawyer, not your spouse.
9. Use the lawyers as hired insulators. Learn to say: "Talk to your lawyer and have him talk to mine."
10. Don't rub in your legal victories. Losers try to even up.

23. What are current trends in divorce law?

Some states are considering or have implemented the following:

1. Minimizing or eliminating the importance of marital misconduct when considering the awarding of alimony (maintenance) and distribution of property. (Note: *Individual judges have almost unlimited discretion in their decisions.* It can be difficult to prove that a judge was prejudiced or influenced by marital misconduct in a particular case.)

13

2. Eliminating existing fault grounds, thus making "the irreconcilable breakdown of the marriage" the sole ground for divorce.

3. A broad, new approach to the resolution or trial of domestic-relations cases, with an emphasis on a tax and business partnership approach as opposed to fault and marital misconduct. Requiring maintenance and child-support payments to be paid directly to an official of the court who is empowered to act immediately when the payor is in arrears. Execution of wage assignments which go into effect only when child support is a month or more in arrears.

4. Requiring a conversion privilege in health-insurance policies for the divorced spouse without proof of insurability.

5. Allowing continuation of group health insurance for divorced spouses or a conversion privilege in health insurance policies without proof of insurability.

6. Recognizing an interest in retirement and pension benefits as an asset subject to claims of the spouse upon divorce.

7. Adopting the Uniform Child Custody Jurisdiction Act (UCCJA) —now the law in some 49 states—which is designed to discourage child-snatching.

8. Passage of the federal Parental Kidnapping Prevention Act. Federal agencies are now available to locate and apprehend child-snatchers.

9. Recognizing the contribution (nonmonetary as well as monetary) of the spouse as homemaker, parent, helper-to-career and well-being of other spouse as factors in determining property distribution and/or maintenance (in 22 states).

10. The use of mediation and arbitration instead of court contests to resolve marital disputes.

11. An increase in joint child custody awards as well as sole custody to fathers.

12. The passage of legislation in 43 states which makes domestic violence a crime or which provides for a variety of remedies, including injunctions, exclusive possession of residences, and imprisonment for violators.

13. The passage of legislation in certain states which makes forced sexual relations by a spouse a crime.

14. Granting visitation rights to grandparents and other third parties with a close connection to children of divorced parents.

CAUTION: Even as this book is being printed, new laws are being passed. Therefore it cannot be overemphasized: check, preferably with a knowledgeable lawyer, *your local laws, customs, and judges,* and ask how these are likely to affect your case.

Chapter **III**

CHOOSING
A LAWYER

24. Can I get a divorce without a lawyer?

In most states, yes. If there are no complications involved and you and your spouse can agree on *every* issue, you can file the necessary papers and enter the final judgment dissolving the marriage.

CAUTION: If you have property to divide, children to provide for, or alimony to pay, you should seek the advice of a lawyer as to rights and responsibilities in those areas.

25. Must the lawyer be a matrimonial specialist?

Not necessarily, but he must be familiar with the matrimonial practice as it is conducted in the *court where your case will be heard.* If your case is simple, with no complex issues or great controversy and no substantial property involved, obviously you have less need for a super-specialist than if your case is potentially complex or contested. A primary function of your lawyer is to give you perspective about the potential results in your case. He must be familiar with the support ranges and property divisions customarily granted in your court at this particular time. Changing laws and changing judges result in changing applications of the law. Your choice is similar to that offered in the medical profession—if you have a difficult medical problem, you will be more likely to go to a specialist than a general practitioner.

If you suspect that your spouse has hired, or will hire, a lawyer with considerable experience who carries a great deal of weight in the court where your case will be heard, you need a lawyer with equal influence. The consideration your case and your lawyer will receive is very often related to the respect your lawyer can command from the court and the opposing lawyer.

CAUTION: A knowledge of tax law is a *must* where property transfers and support payments are involved. You need a divorce lawyer who can foresee potential problems and make their resolution part of the settlement. Outside tax expertise can be called upon to assist in the resolution if necessary.

26. How do I find a lawyer?

There are a number of ways. First, ask for a recommendation from a lawyer you have used—and liked—in the past. If that lawyer does not handle divorce matters, he can refer you to someone who does.

A second source is friends and relatives who have dealt with divorce lawyers. Since no one ever feels like a winner in a matrimonial case, they will frequently refer you to their spouse's lawyer. ("But don't tell him I sent you.") In any event, they can tell you about their own experience with their lawyer and give you some help on what to look for and what to avoid.

A third source of information is the referral services of your state and local bar associations, which are listed in the telephone yellow pages. Tell them it is a matrimonial case and ask for the names of a couple of people experienced in that area of practice.

Since the United States Supreme Court has approved advertising by lawyers, you can now look to your local newspaper or yellow pages to find a lawyer who specializes or concentrates his practice in matrimonial law. Unfortunately, most states do not certify specialists, and there is no way to verify the truth of any particular advertisement without checking out that lawyer's reputation through the bar association or by asking other lawyers or friends who have dealt with that person. *A lawyer's reputation among other lawyers is probably the most valid indication of his capabilities.*

27. What if my spouse suggests a lawyer?

Be careful. It is not likely your spouse wants you to have the best divorce lawyer in town—or even the fifteenth best! On the other hand, if you have checked out a particular lawyer who seems right for you, don't eliminate him just because of your spouse's recommendation. That could have been the reason for the recommendation in the first place.

28. Can one lawyer represent both of us?

One lawyer can never really represent both parties in a matrimonial action if there are any disputed issues, but it is not always necessary to have two lawyers. If the matter is simple and there are no contested issues, one of the parties can appear "pro se," that is, represent himself. One lawyer draws all the necessary documents and proceeds with the dissolution without the necessity of a second lawyer. You can then share the cost of that lawyer's services.

CAUTION: If regular support payments, questions over custody or visitation of children, or division of property are involved, you should at least have a second lawyer look over the agreement before you sign it. A small change in the weekly support rate can mean thousands of dollars over an extended period of time. A misunderstanding about your interest in marital property could result in an unforeseen tax obligation, and so on. In only the simplest cases should you take the chance of going it alone—and perhaps not even then.

29. Should I shop for a lawyer?

Yes, unless you have a referral source in whom you are totally confident. For example, if you have a great deal of trust in your business lawyer, and he makes a very strong recommendation, follow it unless the other indicators are negative. Otherwise, interview at least two or more lawyers and compare them in terms of competence, personality, and price. The personality factor is important because you will have to deal closely with this individual on potentially volatile problems. While you needn't be totally enchanted, a clash of personalities may make this relationship uncomfortable or even contentious. If your case is a simple one, you may wish to avoid the lawyer who appears unnecessarily contentious. The key test in judging your lawyer's personality is simply compatibility with your own—or at least an absence of *incompatibility.*

30. What about law clinics or publicly supported legal services?

Law clinics are a comparatively new development in the law practice. The quality of service of any particular clinic in the matrimonial area will depend on the lawyers and supportive personnel involved. If you interview at such a clinic, your price criterion will probably be met, but you still must consider the lawyer's competence and personality. After your initial interview, if you are satisfied on those points, there is no reason not to hire the lawyer. However, ask whether that lawyer will be the person representing you, or whether it will be an associate or other office personnel. If your case requires personal attention, then you want to know who will be giving you that attention.

The fact that a clinic may advertise divorce for $250 does not mean it won't be entitled to a larger fee if there is a great deal of personal contact and litigation time involved in your case. These matters should be clarified at the outset of your relationship with the law clinic or with any other law office. The difference between law clinics and private offices is that lawyers in the clinic attempt to minimize *their* hours spent with the client. They maximize the use of forms and the assistance of secretaries and paralegals who charge at a lesser rate because they do not have law degrees. This approach is satisfactory if the case is simple and does not involve a lot of contact between lawyer and client.

Ask about the hourly charge for the *lawyer* at the clinic. Compare that rate with what is commonly charged in your community and determine whether the clinic is a bargain for *you*.

31. What do I need to know for my initial interview with the lawyer?

Ideally, you should be prepared to describe the extent and value of your property, your monthly living expenses, and the amount of available income. (See the Initial Interview Information Sheet on page 139.)

If this information is not immediately available to you, it can be furnished later, and the interview need not be delayed in the meantime.

CAUTION: The lawyer can only advise and predict on the information *you* furnish at this stage of the case. The more incomplete the information, the more vague the advice.

32. Is my interview confidential?

Yes, even if you do not hire that lawyer. Laws and rules of ethics recognize a lawyer-client privilege that prohibits the lawyer from divulging information learned when acting as a lawyer, unlike what is heard in a casual conversation at a cocktail party. Because of that privilege and the confidential nature of your interview, this lawyer will probably be disqualified from representing your spouse if you do not hire him. Some people have been known to interview the top matrimonial lawyers in their area in order to disqualify them as potential representatives of their spouse in later matrimonial litigation.

CAUTION: If your attorney discusses other cases with you in intimate detail or identifies litigants in discussions at cocktail parties or other social events, and if confidentiality is important to you, he is probably not for you. Competent matrimonial lawyers are not gossips.

33. What should I expect of my lawyer in handling my divorce case?

Your lawyer should help you maintain perspective as to what is a fair settlement. He or she should assist you in discovering all the assets and income information necessary to arrive at such a settlement. He should be prepared to litigate issues that cannot be resolved by agreement, either due to the arbitrary position of the other side or the inability to agree on certain factual questions. You should also expect the lawyer to at least partially *control* the case. He should control you in order to avoid willful violations of court orders or agreements. He should control the opposition by frustrating attempts to take advantage of you by willful or arbitrary conduct. By controlling you and the litigation, the lawyer ultimately presents you with certain settlement options. You have been well represented if you have options to choose from rather than results forced upon you.

Few matrimonial cases are definitive victories or losses. The grays predominate over blacks and whites, and your lawyer prepares you to accept the grays. (And perhaps saves you money in the process.)

Don't expect a miracle or even a stunning victory. The competent lawyer looks for a fair settlement rather than a punitive one. Beware of the lawyer who encourages your desire to get revenge upon your spouse by financial or other means. Also beware of the lawyer who promises you everything. In the emotional context of a marital dispute, you are at the lowest ebb in your ability to make reasonable judgments. If the lawyer gets caught up in your emotionalism, his judgment will be no better than your own. One clear head is better than none.

19

QUESTIONS TO ASK YOUR LAWYER
AT THE INITIAL INTERVIEW

1. What percentage of the lawyer's practice involves matrimonial cases?
2. Does the lawyer have trial experience in matrimonial cases?
3. Is the lawyer willing to go to court to litigate the case if it cannot be settled?
4. Will the lawyer handle the case personally or will an associate in his office handle it? (If another person in the office is to be involved, you may wish to have an interview with that associate prior to retaining the lawyer.)
5. What is the lawyer's procedure for telephoning him at his home?
6. How long will it take to resolve your suit *after* an agreement is reached? How long will it take if any matter is severely contested? (In most cases, the lawyer will only be able to give you a general estimate because he cannot control court calendars or the other side's determination either to cooperate or stall the resolution of the case.)
7. What will the lawyer expect from you in terms of assistance in the discovery process and in terms of availability for court hearings, conferences, or depositions?
8. On what basis does the lawyer charge for his services in matrimonial matters? If he uses an hourly rate, what is that rate for office time and for court time?
9. Does the lawyer consider his fees to be average in your community, or above or below average?

34. What if I don't feel comfortable with the lawyer after the initial interview?

That lawyer is not for you and should not be hired. Your time will not have been wasted, because you will have a clearer idea of what you are looking for when you interview the next lawyer. Remember, the initial interview is a two-way street. The lawyer is also deciding whether or not he wants your case. You have every right to be as selective. If you are not comfortable with a particular lawyer, or if you question his competence, you will never fully trust him, and his ability to represent you effectively will be undermined.

10. What does the lawyer estimate the court costs will be?
11. Which spouse will be liable for the fees and court costs? How will that liability be determined?
12. Does the lawyer charge a retainer fee? How much will it be and is it refundable in full or in part under any circumstances?
13. Can the lawyer give a ball-park estimate on the total fee?
14. Will there be monthly billings or will the fee be due at some particular time?
15. Will there be charges for outside services by accountants or investigators? Does the lawyer charge *extra* for work by his paralegals or secretaries?
16. Present company excepted, who does the lawyer consider to be the best qualified matrimonial lawyers in your area? (Only ask this question if you are shopping. It is useful if you find that the same name or names come up repeatedly.)
17. Based on the information you have given him, ask the lawyer what results he would anticipate on any particular contested issue in your case either by court decision or by negotiation. (Since predictions are risky and the information you have provided is probably incomplete, you should expect a guarded answer with no absolute assurances of a particular result.)
18. If you are satisfied with the answers to the previous questions, then ask the following: How do local laws affect any issues which may be contested in your case relating to child custody, support, alimony, or property division?
19. Ask any personal questions you have regarding your rights and responsibilities in connection with your spouse, e.g., whether you must prepare meals, pay your spouse's charge accounts, file joint tax returns, etc.

35. What criteria do I use to compare lawyers in order to choose one to represent me?

The lawyer's answers to the Questions to Ask Your Lawyer at the Initial Interview on page 20 will aid you in judging his suitability based on knowledge and experience. Your reaction to the lawyer as a person is equally important, because you will ultimately have to trust his judgment. It is hard to trust someone if you have a negative reaction to his personality.

36. At what point is the lawyer retained?

When you ask the lawyer to represent you and he accepts. If the acceptance of that responsibility is conditioned upon your payment of a retainer fee, then his responsibility does not begin until that fee is paid.

LAWYERS' FEES AND COURT COSTS

37. How important is cost in choosing a lawyer?

Lawyers have only so many hours a day to devote to their law practice, so the lawyers who are in greater demand generally charge more for their time. Price is not always a measure of competence, however. In every community there are lawyers whose achievements in public relations exceed their legal skills, who charge more than they are worth. You must first learn the ball-park figure for your type of divorce. (The case where both parties agree is the cheapest, and the contested-through-trial case the most expensive.) Friends who have recently been through a divorce, or else the local bar association, can tell you what the going rate is. If a lawyer you are considering charges substantially above *or* below the average figure in your community, you should explore that lawyer's credentials further before hiring him. Although some of the most competent lawyers may only charge in the average fee range, few undercharge. A lawyer charging substantially below the norm may lack experience in the matrimonial field.

To put it another way, some of the best fee bargains in the matrimonial field come from young lawyers who make up in

22

dedication what they lack in experience. However, if your case is likely to involve lengthy negotiations and a complicated settlement, or may go to trial, you should not take a chance on inexperience. In the long run, if you can afford the more expensive lawyer who has a good reputation in the matrimonial field, you are probably wise to spend the money. His stature in your local legal community may have a significant effect on the outcome of your case.

38. How do lawyers charge in matrimonial cases?

Most lawyers charge a retainer fee (see Question 42) for taking a case and charge additional fees as the case proceeds or at the conclusion of the case. The retainer can run from a few hundred to several thousand dollars, depending on the lawyer's reputation in your community and the anticipated difficulty of your case. Most lawyers keep track of the hours they spend on a case and bill accordingly. Before retaining a lawyer, you should determine the amount of his retainer fee and the hourly rate that he charges if you are to be billed on a time basis as well. When a lawyer represents a woman whose husband is the breadwinner, he may frequently require her to pay only the retainer fee, with the understanding that the balance of fees will come from the husband. The lawyer may nevertheless keep track of his time in order to justify the fee charged to the husband. As women have gained greater economic independence, there has been a trend around the country to require the husband to pay a lesser share of the wife's lawyer's fees and costs. In most cases, if you decide to fire your attorney, the retainer fee will *not* be refunded, and additional fees will be required if the time already spent on the case justifies it. Hourly rates for matrimonial lawyers will vary substantially, but fees from $50 to $150 an hour are not at all uncommon, and recognized specialists may charge more. In New York City, for example, the fee might go as high as $300 an hour.

39. May I ask the lawyer's fee on the telephone when I make my initial appointment?

Yes, but don't be surprised if he refuses to quote a fee until he has more information about your case. Some lawyers or the secretary with whom you make the initial appointment do quote minimum fees and hourly rates, and you should not hesitate to ask. However, the fact that information is not given over the telephone should not keep you from making an appointment. If you are looking for the cheapest possible divorce, the best lawyers will probably not be interested in your case anyway.

40. Do I have to pay for the initial interview with the lawyer?

Because this varies, you should ask when setting your appointment. Many competent and highly regarded lawyers do not charge for initial interviews. If it is clear, however, at your initial interview that you are *not* looking for a lawyer to *hire*, but are seeking legal *information*, the lawyer probably will charge for his time and you should be willing to pay for it.

41. Do I discuss fees at the initial interview?

Definitely. If the information is not offered by the lawyer, you should ask him what his retainer fee will be, whether or not it is refundable, and whether he will be charging you at an hourly rate or on some other basis. Bar associations no longer have minimum-fee schedules, but all lawyers have their own criteria, which generally include a minimum fee and an hourly rate of charge.

COMMENT: Many good lawyers are more uncomfortable discussing fees than their clients. The fact that *you* have to bring up the subject does not necessarily mean he intends to charge a fortune.

42. What is a retainer fee?

This is the fee a lawyer initially charges for taking your case. It is generally not the entire fee. Hours spent on your case may be credited against the retainer fee. If the cost of the divorce goes beyond the initial retainer amount (as it usually does), the succeeding hours are added on to be paid in the manner previously agreed upon.

The retainer is normally not refundable if you reconcile or seek to hire new counsel unless the fee was substantial and essentially no services were performed. In that event, a large retainer would be an "unconscionable fee," which is forbidden by the Code of Professional Responsibility governing the conduct of lawyers in most states.

43. What are court costs?

In a strict sense, court costs are only those charges made by the court in connection with the filing of the case or subsequent pleadings, and for transcribing the record of court proceedings. In a more general sense, court costs include any costs incurred in your suit other than compensation for the lawyer. This would include investigative fees, court-reporter charges for depositions, subpoena

24

fees, photocopy costs, postage, telephone, and the like. Most lawyers keep track of the costs separately from their fees and present them to you in an itemized bill. When the attorney quotes you a fee, he does not normally include these costs.

44. Should I have a written contract with the lawyer?

If there is a fixed overall fee arrangement or a strict hourly-rate charge, a contract indicating the amount of the fees or hourly rates as well as the *specific* services to be performed is desirable. Even a letter or memorandum from the lawyer setting forth the services which he intends to perform, and whatever fee information he can provide, is a good idea if no formal contract is drawn. This is a protection to the lawyer as well as the client because the emotional turmoil of matrimonial litigation often undermines the relationship between lawyer and client. The lawyer may want to remove himself from the case later on or the client may want to discharge the lawyer, and it is helpful to have some memorandum that will eliminate any question as to the initial fee arrangement. Lawyers frequently insist on such a memorandum if the case appears potentially troublesome at the outset.

CHILD CUSTODY

45. When do we tell the children about the divorce?

As soon as you feel that it is inevitable. Don't be surprised if they already know. In the case of a separation, the children should be told at or about the time it occurs. The key word is honesty. Don't hold out false hopes that the marital relationship will continue if it is obvious that it will not. Don't blame your spouse for everything, but also make it clear that the separation is in no way the children's fault. Children frequently blame themselves for their parents' marital problems.

Consult sources in the Bibliography that refer to children and divorce. If you feel unequal to the task, don't hesitate to seek advice from a therapist. Take advantage of the guidance available for you and your child during a period when you both may need it most.

46. How do we tell the children?

Keep it simple and straightforward.

Both of you should tell your children at the same time if your relationship allows that kind of cooperation.

26

Don't dramatize or become sentimental.

Avoid an air of remorse or devastation.

If you and your spouse have been fighting openly for some time, the kids may even be relieved that the truth is out—and that the arguments and tension will stop.

Reassure them that you both love them.

Let them have their say—tears, anger, hurt, pleadings.

Let them know with whom and where they will live if that is agreed. If it isn't, both of you should try to encourage them to express what they want, while making it clear that they will not have the burden of choosing or rejecting a parent.

Do not make promises or hold out false hopes of reconciliation.

If there is likely to be a contest over custody or grounds, assure the children they will not have to be involved in the court proceedings—if that is the case. All children tend to be apprehensive on this point.

Do not in any way encourage them to take sides. Eventually, you will have an ex-wife or ex-husband, but your children will not have an ex-mother or ex-father.

Assure the children that you both will always be there when you are needed—if that is the truth.

Read some helpful books on the subject. (See the Bibliography.) Get professional help for any child who appears unable to cope with the stress.

47. Do mothers always get custody of children?

No. Although traditionally it was presumed that young children were better off living with their mother, most states have rejected this as a fast rule and many more fathers now seek custody of their children. A mother now must prove that she is in fact the principal nurturing parent, or that, for some other reason, the children would best be served by being placed in her custody.

A father seeking custody has the same burden of proof. With the change in traditional male and female roles over the years and the increase in career opportunities for women, it is no longer unusual for the father to be the principal nurturing parent, both psychologically and physically. In the great majority of custody cases, it is the past history of caring for the children rather than any sudden rush to become a super-parent during the divorce proceedings which the court will consider in making its custodial determination. A parent who has been indifferent or neglectful isn't going to convince the court by suddenly becoming attentive and loving.

Today, more fathers are being awarded custody by the courts, sometimes with the mother's agreement, sometimes against her wishes. If a mother, for example, leaves the state or lives with someone to whom she is not married, or if she is giving her career priority over care of the children, she may lose custody if the husband appears able and willing to act as the principal caretaker.

48. How do I know whether there will be a custody fight?

One of you probably was principally responsible for the day-to-day care of the children. This person, in most cases, would be expected to be the custodian. On the other hand, the question of custody is often used as a smoke screen behind which other issues are negotiated. The worst kind of court battles can result. The children may be used as leverage to achieve an advantage in some other area of dispute such as alimony or property division.

An even worse battle results when a parent contests custody to gain revenge upon the spouse for an unwanted marital breakup. This is striking where it hurts the most without regard to the effect on the children. Greed can at least be bought off with settlement concessions. Self-righteousness almost always leads to an expensive trial where the results may be harsher than either party anticipated.

49. Can the children be used as witnesses?

Yes. If they are mature enough to give reliable testimony, the children are considered legally competent to testify both as to grounds and custodial issues. Whether or not they *should* be used as witnesses is another question. The parent who wants a child to testify, or threatens to use the child as a witness, is not giving first priority to the welfare of the child. Testimony in open court or even in the judge's chambers, where it is most often heard, is traumatic to any child, at almost any age. The mere suggestion that the child might have to testify against a parent creates a state of apprehension which may not end until long after the divorce is over. The parent may not be aware of that apprehension because it is often unspoken. Every effort should be made to complete litigation without using the children as witnesses. They should be assured on this point from the outset to avoid unnecessary fears.

50. What is joint custody?

Joint custory is an award of the child's legal custody to *both* parents, with specific provision made for his or her principal place of residence. Legal custody is the right to make vital decisions regarding a child's education, religious training, health care, and the like. While joint custody was only occasionally used in the past, more than 24 states have now enacted legislation allowing some form of joint parenting on the dissolution of a marriage. In some states, joint custody is an option available only by agreement. In others, it is the presumed or preferred arrangement.

Many child psychologists and domestic-relations specialists discourage joint custody because it can result in a conflict of parental authority, with parents and children in a continuous battle for affection or control. Joint custody can work if *both* parents are more interested in the *children's* best interests than in their own rights. Most divorced people cannot sustain a sufficient degree of cooperation to keep personal antagonism out of this less-structured custodial arrangement. Notwithstanding the potential problems, there is a definite trend to joint custody, and bills have been introduced in every state legislature calling for some form of joint parenting.

51. What is split custody?

Split custody is an arrangement whereby the children live each (or some) with a different parent, or all together with each parent for a portion of the year.

The split-year arrangement is most common when the parents live so far apart that frequent contact for short periods is impractical. The disadvantage is the difficulty the children may experience in adjusting to a new school and social environment every few months.

Splitting the children is usually done only when the children clearly prefer it. The mutually supportive relationship of siblings can provide continuity and stability when the parents have separated. Those benefits should not be sacrificed as a negotiation compromise or to suit parental convenience.

52. Can the children choose with whom they want to live?

Before any formal court hearing, the parents should give serious consideration to the preference of the children. Most parents are not inclined to *force* a child to live with them. On the other hand, if a child's preference is expressed in court, it will be weighed in light of the child's maturity and the reasons for the preference. There is no set age at which a child's preference will *control* the court's determination. It is only one of many factors to be taken into consideration in determining *the best interests of the child*, the universal standard for custodial awards.

53. Should we ask the children with whom they prefer to live?

If they have not voluntarily expressed a preference, the children are probably telling you that they do not want to make the decision. In that case, it is better not to ask directly. However, there are many ways to indirectly explore a child's preference. For example, if separation and divorce are inevitable, the father may discuss his own future living arrangements with the children. To observe their reactions, he might talk about a room that could be set aside for them. Unless a child is severely repressed, he will generally say how he sees himself in the separated arrangement.

Don't try to manipulate the child's opinion by seducing him with promises of an unreal environment of fun and games. Don't create a dependency relationship or try to make the child feel sorry for you. The mother who says, "Who will take care of me if you don't live with me?" or the father who says, "I guess you will never see me again after the divorce," is in effect trying to manipulate the child into expressing a custodial preference out of pity. If he chooses to live with the pitiful parent, the child often plays the part of parent and assumes many burdens which are inappropriate to his age or stage of development. Parents who give the children's welfare first priority will not place any of these false expectations or burdens on a child in an effort to influence the choice of custodian.

Bear in mind that, even at its most amiable, divorce is hard on children. They may not *know* whom they want to live with, they may not want to be asked, they may change their minds, they may continue to hope their parents will get together again.

54. How do courts rule on temporary custody?

The child's best interest is the test for temporary custody, the same as in a final hearing. Generally the temporary-motion judge does not have time to grant a full hearing, and the tendency is to leave the child where he is until a final and complete hearing. If both of the parents are in the home, the child remains with both. If one of the parents has moved out, the child generally remains with the parent who is in the home. Normally a child has strong ties to school, friends, and activities in that neighborhood, and removal would cause a serious disruption. On the other hand, if there is evidence of potential harm to the child if left with a particular parent, courts will usually grant a hearing on that issue and order temporary custody accordingly.

55. May I leave the state with the children?

Yes, if there is no custody action pending or decree entered. Otherwise, it will be necessary for you to obtain court permission or the approval of your spouse before removing the children from the jurisdiction. That approval should be in writing because the spouse who says yes today may deny it tomorrow after you have left, and you will incur substantial litigation costs as a result.

If your spouse does not agree to your leaving the state, petition the court. If there is a valid reason for leaving, such as remarriage, an improved employment opportunity, or a health condition, and the removal is in the child's best interests, the court may grant permission to leave, with new arrangements made for visitation. Support arrangements can also be altered to accommodate the additional expense of transporting the child for visitation.

If the children are being taken out of the state to keep a parent from visiting or some other reason not in the children's interest the petition to remove may be denied. On the other hand, reduction of visitation time is generally not a sufficient basis for denying the petition to remove.

56. What if the custodian takes the children to live out of state without permission or court order?

A petition should be filed immediately in the court where the last custody order was entered, asking that the children be returned to their home state and that a contempt citation be issued against the parent removing the children. A delay in filing this petition may suggest that you are indifferent or in agreement with the removal and will give the custodial parent an opportunity to establish a new home state for the children. The court will be reluctant to remove them from the new home if it has been established for six months or more without formal protest by the noncustodian.

Most state courts will allow the custodian to remove a child from the state for good cause, and custody will not be changed solely because a child has been removed without permission. If home-state orders to return the child are ignored, you will have to go to the state where the child is living to enforce your order. Disputes between state courts over the custody of children are common, but all states are now required to follow the jurisdictional guidelines of the Uniform Child Custody Jurisdiction Act.

57. What if the noncustodial parent takes the children to live out of state without permission?

If the children are not promptly returned, and you are unable to go to where they are living and bring them back, file an *immediate* petition for contempt of court. Your spouse has "snatched" the children and is subject to fine or imprisonment for a willful violation of the custody judgment.

If the contempt proceedings in your state are ignored by your spouse, you will have to go to the state where he or she is living to enforce your custody rights.

58. How are conflicts between different state courts over the custody of children resolved?

Although the United States Constitution requires all states to give full faith and credit to the valid judgments of other states, this does not always happen in the case of custody disputes. Because each state takes jurisdiction over the children within its borders, and because any custody judgments can be modified on proof of a substantial change of circumstances, custody issues are frequently, and unfortunately, relitigated as the children are moved from state to state.

To avoid these unsettling and expensive conflicts of laws, most states have enacted some form of the Uniform Child Custody Jurisdiction Act, which is designed to resolve interstate custody jurisdiction. The Act sets forth rules to determine which state should properly have jurisdiction to decide a custody dispute and provides rules for the transfer of witnesses, social-service investigative reports, and other evidence between state courts. By promoting cooperation among state courts, the Act should end the gamesmanship between warring parents who move from state to state to seek favorable custodial decisions or to avoid the orders of a prior home state. Once states to which children are brought refuse to relitigate custody disputes and order children returned to their home state, the child-snatching epidemic we are now seeing should be eliminated.

The federal Parental Kidnapping Prevention Act, which became effective in 1981, requires that all state courts follow the jurisdictional standards of the Uniform Child Custody Jurisdiction Act. The federal law also makes available a parent-locater service to track down kidnapping parents. The Act directs the Justice Departmen to assist in the apprehension of parents if they violated state felony laws in removing a child to another state.

Chapter **VI**

CHILD SUPPORT
AND VISITATION

59. How is the amount of child support determined?

To establish the amount of child support, the actual needs of
the children must be proved, as well as the parents' income and
assets. The courts generally deal in net income, that is, income
after the deduction of taxes, Social Security, mandatory pension
contributions, union dues, insurance payments, and the like. Since
child-support orders entered against the noncustodial parent rarely
cover all the needs of the children, the custodian will have to
contribute to maintaining the household as well. Both parents'
incomes will be taken into consideration in determining amounts.
Some typical child-support schedules of various courts have been
included on page 142 to provide an idea of support ranges commonly used at particular income levels. In most jurisdictions these
schedules are only guidelines, and court orders will vary according
to the particular needs in each case.

60. Will child-support payments cover my total financial obligation to the children?

In addition to child-support payments, the children are also entitled to ask for college expenses and extraordinary medical, dental and hospitalization payments, life insurance, health insurance and, in some states, support after the death of the supporting parent in the form of a probate estate claim.

The financially obligated parent is usually required to maintain health insurance for the children when it is available at a place of employment and some amount of life insurance geared to the children's standard of living and the number of years until they come of age.

The college-expense requirement is usually limited to four years of undergraduate education or similar trade-school training after high school. The amount the noncustodial parent usually has to contribute takes into consideration the financial means of both parents as well as any assets of the children.

In some states the duty to support children is not terminated upon death, and the custodial parent may make a claim in the divorce court for support from the estate of a deceased parent, either in periodic payments or in a lump sum.

Even if your decree doesn't provide for any of the extra child support listed above, you are entitled to apply to the court for such support when the need arises.

61. Can I get child custody and support even though we are not divorced and there is no divorce suit pending?

Most states allow the filing of an action for custody and support of children, or for visitation, without the necessity of filing for divorce or legal separation. Every state has jurisdiction over the children within its borders, even if there is not a specific statute for custody or visitation or support suits. Where there is no pending action or judgment already entered in connection with custody or visitation, both parents have an equal right to have the children reside with them.

62. When a spouse remarries, is the new spouse's income taken into account when determining child support?

Technically, no. The new spouse has no obligation to support someone else's children. As a practical matter, however, the fact that a new spouse may be paying a lot of the household expenses is relevant in determining how much the noncustodial parent has available for support payments or how much the custodian needs for the children. For example, if the custodian mother was paying $500 monthly rent until she remarried and moved into her new husband's home rent-free, this is a relevant *need* consideration. Similarly, if a new wife applies her income to household expenses, her husband's *ability* to pay child support increases. Generally speaking, though, courts will not increase or decrease child support based solely on the income of the new spouse.

63. Can a claim, in the event of death, be written into the divorce decree?

Yes, either in the form of a fixed dollar amount or a percentage of the estate. The more common arrangement, however, is to specify a life-insurance obligation payable to the children. The payment in the event of death is quicker, simpler and more certain. Support and alimony claims in the event of death can also be drafted as part of an estate plan that will reduce death taxes. In states which have adopted some form of the Uniform Marriage and Divorce Act, claims for continuing child support can be filed *after* the death of a supporting parent.

64. Must I pay support if my spouse is not allowing visitation, or must I allow visitation if my spouse is not paying support?

Yes, you must, unless a court order has been entered modifying your visitation or support obligation. The right of visitation and the duty to pay support are completely separate, and the court will enforce both independently. Some states have statutes, however, which allow the suspension of support if the custodial parent is willfully interfering with visitation rights. The suspension cannot be made unilaterally, as a court hearing must first be conducted to see if the visitation abuse is willful. In any case, a petition for contempt should be filed promptly with the court if support or visitation provisions are regularly violated.

In keeping with the separation of questions of support and visitation, it is also important not to pay support or discuss money in connection with picking up the children for visitation or returning them. The children undergo enough stress when a marital breakdown occurs and should not have visitation associated with money problems.

65. How are orders for visitation or support enforced?

You must file a petition for enforcement or similar proceeding in the court where your divorce is pending or where the divorce decree was entered. If the custodial or support parent is living in another state, that state will also enforce your visitation or support order if you file a petition there.

Another means of obtaining child support when the paying parent lives in another state is through the Uniform Reciprocal Enforcement Support Act, which is administered by your local district attorney. The advantage of this procedure is that it is free (no lawyer's fee or court costs), and you don't have to go to the other state. The disadvantage is that child support is the only relief obtainable, and a new support order will be entered that may be less favorable than what you had under your divorce decree. Nonsupport actions can also be brought in your local criminal court, but you will probably achieve better collection through the divorce court.

Many states now provide for support enforcement at no charge through the Friend of the Court or state's attorney. These programs usually involve support payments directly to the court clerk, who records and distributes them to the recipient. The transactions are computerized and arrearage notices and enforcement proceedings are often automatic.

Another development in support enforcement is the automatic wage assignment. Recent legislation in a few states requires that all supporting parents execute a wage assignment at the time the support order is entered. The wage assignment automatically goes into effect if the supporting parent falls thirty or sixty days in arrears on the support payments. Thereafter, the current support and arrearages are automatically deducted from the supporting parent's wages until the arrearage is made up or until further order of the court.

An increasing number of support deadbeats is a national problem, and a serious effort is being made by state legislatures and governmental agencies to provide more aggressive child-support enforcement at the state's expense. Visitation problems may not be as widespread as those relating to support, but enforcement can be just as difficult where the custodial parent undermines the visitation orders.

66. What is reasonable visitation?

Reasonable visitation describes a noncustodial parent's visiting rights, when specific times are not detailed in the agreement or decree. The term implies a mutual understanding as to what is expected in terms of periods of visitation and will, therefore, vary with each family. Note the sample visitation schedules on the following page to compare very light visitation with very extensive visitation schedules. Any combination of these paragraph can be

36

used to tailor your visitation provisions if what the parent considers "reasonable" is not satisfactory.

CAUTION: If you and your spouse cannot agree what is "reasonable," then it is definitely recommended that you have the specific periods of visitation spelled out in the decree. (See the sample visitation provisions on the following page.)

67. When should the children meet the new girl/boy friend?

Take your time. If you're still married and your spouse is likely to be hostile to "exposing" the children to your friend, then save them from the additional pressure of dealing with your new relationship. The children will generally reflect the attitude of your spouse toward marital "rivals." Let them adjust to the reality of your divorce before forcing a meeting with someone they may resent out of jealousy or loyalty to their other parent. When the children *want* to meet your friend you'll know it, and that's the best time. In the meanwhile, resist the temptation to involve the children in this new relationship, which may, in fact, only be temporary.

68. What can be done about the child who refuses to visit?

Not much. Hostility between parents is often behind the child's reluctance. Forcing the child, either by the parent's pressure or by court orders, only intensifies the problem. Even if the custodial parent is the proven culprit in discouraging visitation, the child will probably resent the imposition of court sanctions. Patience and psychological counseling are the only hope for altering the child's attitude. It is not uncommon for the child to outgrow this kind of reluctance and even to reject the parent who was encouraging it.

69. Can children have their own lawyers?

Yes. Sometimes parents and their lawyers lose sight of a child's best interest in their zeal to "win." Where that is the case, the child should have his own attorney.

In an increasing number of states, it is the regular practice to appoint a guardian or a lawyer for the children to represent their interests in custody litigation. The guardian-lawyer usually conducts an investigation into the child's home environment and explores particular issues raised by the parents as being favorable to their case. The lawyer then reports back either to the court or to the lawyers for the parties and sometimes makes a recommendation as to the best temporary or permanent arrangement for the child.

VISITATION PROVISIONS—SAMPLE

Light visitation schedule:

The father/mother shall have the right to visit* with the minor children on alternate Saturdays and Sundays, on alternate national holidays, and for an extended period during the children's summer vacation.

Average visitation schedule:

The father/mother shall visit with the minor children on alternate weekends from Saturday at (10 A.M.) until Sunday at (7 P.M.) and one evening per week for dinner. In addition, the father/mother shall visit on alternate national and religious holidays, to wit: Christmas Day, New Year's Day, Easter Sunday, Memorial Day, Fourth of July, Labor Day, and Thanksgiving. The holiday visitation shall be from 9 A.M. to 8 P.M. When the holiday occurs on a Monday, the children shall be with the father/mother the preceding weekend, notwithstanding the provision for alternate weekend visitation. In addition, the father/mother shall have visitation for one half the Christmas vacation, alternate spring vacations and for four weeks during the children's summer vacation.

Extraordinary visitation:

The father/mother shall have visitation with the children every weekend from Friday after school until Sunday evening; on alternate national and religious holidays (see above) for one half of the Christmas vacation; for all of the spring vacation, and for six weeks during the summer. The father/mother shall also have the right to take the children out to dinner two nights per week and to contact them at least once per day by telephone.

* This does *not* mean visit in the custodial parent's home. In most cases visits are specifically *not* in that home.

The weight given to this recommendation by the court is generally substantial. The guardian has a great deal of influence in determining who is given custody because he is considered to be impartial and is concerned only with the best interests of his client, the child. The impartial opinion of the child's representative, after a thorough investigation, often results in a custody settlement without trial, since both lawyers understand that the court is most likely to follow his or her recommendations. Face-saving compromises are reached, and a lot of expense and acrimony is thus avoided.

70. What may be involved in the guardian-lawyer's investigation and representation of the children?

Interviews with the children.
Interviews with parents or potential custodians.
Interviews with teachers, neighbors, and other knowledgeable third parties.
Investigation of the home and neighborhood.
Examination of school and medical records.
Suggesting psychological evaluations or treatment for children or their parents.
Conducting or attending depositions.
Filing motions on behalf of the children regarding visitation, abuse, health or other problems that the parents haven't called to the attention of the court or been able to resolve themselves.
Filing a report of the investigation (optional).
Attendance in court during trial and preliminary motions.
Making recommendations (optional) to the court or counsel for the parents on a variety of matters dealing with the children, including custody and visitation.
Protecting the children's financial interest in connection with support, health and educational expenses, and seeking a portion of the parents' estate in the event of death or as security for support payments.

71. Who pays the guardian-lawyer's fees and costs?

Either or both parents, depending on their respective financial ability. A child's assets can also be applied to the cost of his representation.

FINANCIAL HIDE-AND-SEEK WITH YOUR SPOUSE

72. Should I close bank accounts?

This is a legitimate act of self-protection if you are able and willing to account for the withdrawn money. If you dissipate it or cannot prove how you spent it, you may delay the settlement of your case and encourage counter-gamesmanship by your spouse.

CAUTION: What starts out as an act of self-protection may escalate into a full-scale war of hide-and-seek. Store your grandmother's silver flatware in your friend's attic if you feel you must, but be prepared to account for its whereabouts, and don't be surprised if the antique clock disappears from the mantel.

73. What should I do about safe-deposit boxes?

If the boxes are joint, at least inventory the contents. If self-protection requires safekeeping until injunctive protection has been obtained, place the contents in another box or some other safe place. In any event, have a neutral third party present when you inventory the box, because you can expect your spouse to

40

claim that your accounting of the contents was not complete. The neutral third party can initial your inventory and verify its accuracy at a later date. A bank employee will be more credible than a friend or relative as your witness.

74. What if there is not enough money to support two families?

This is true in the majority of marital separations. The separated families often have to live at a lower standard than when they lived together because basic living costs are doubled. There may be increased pressure because a spouse who works two or more jobs or regularly does overtime work frequently will drop the extra work because the added income will be computed as a factor in any support order. The money crunch is normally tightest during the divorce when new costs are being encountered and income is being strategically suppressed. Part of the strategy may be to force an unemployed spouse to get a job, and in many cases the employment of both spouses is a necessity if the separated families are to survive.

75. What do I do first to protect myself financially?

If you haven't already done so for the preliminary interview, start gathering information regarding income and assets so that you and your lawyer can budget projected needs for yourself and other members of the family. This effort becomes part of what is called the "discovery procedure." (See also Chapter X, Discovery Procedures.)

1. First determine what property you own, when it was acquired and how, its value, and how title is held. (The Asset/Liability Worksheet on page 157 will assist you.)

2. Determine the actual physical whereabouts of assets and title documents. If you own stock, note where the certificates are kept, where the passbooks for savings accounts are, as well as deeds and other records regarding real estate, etc.

3. If property is missing, or you suspect your spouse may have acquired property without your knowledge, make note of these facts and call them to your lawyer's attention. (The hiding of assets and convenient memory lapses are common behavior for otherwise honest spouses when a divorce is imminent. Review the Hidden Asset Check List on page 49 to assist you in your search.)

Once you know the nature and extent of your assets, and their physical location, you and your lawyer are in a much better position to obtain a fair property division and support agreement.

CAUTION: Discuss with your lawyer what original documents

such as bearer bonds, canceled checks or savings-account pass-books you should hold in safekeeping. Find out if some documents should be copied and replaced without the knowledge of your spouse. If they are later hidden, altered, or disappear you can use that dishonesty as a leverage factor to your own advantage.

76. What will the court do if I hide or spend marital assets?

It is one thing to hide assets and not admit they exist. It is quite another to merely put the assets in safekeeping or use them for necessaries. For example, if you remove funds from a joint bank account and hold them in your own name, or place joint stock certificates in your own safe-deposit box, there is no problem as long as you admit their existence. The judge will not be concerned if the assets are available for division and distribution.

On the other hand, if you claim you lost the money from a joint account at the race track, the judge may assume you are lying even if it is true. The judge may award you the *missing* assets and award an equal amount of the remaining assets to your spouse.

If you can prove that certain assets were spent for a good purpose, such as the payment of family debts or legitimate living expenses, there will probably be no penalty, unless the expenditure was in violation of a court restraining order.

CAUTION: Men or women who are the principal source of family income should consider satisfying outstanding debts from family assets *before* restraining orders are entered. Since you will probably have to pay these debts anyhow, you might as well get contribution from your spouse by using marital or joint assets.

77. What should I do about charge accounts?

Since both spouses are legally liable for balances due on joint charge accounts, your decision to close them depends on how much you *trust* your spouse. If he or she has a history of financial irresponsibility, or if there is a likelihood of vindictiveness, you should probably terminate these accounts. If you have no such fear, leave joint accounts in status quo to avoid recriminations from what your spouse may consider an aggressive or threatening act.

78. Will I be liable for my spouse's charges?

You are liable for family debts if you actually contracted for the debt, or if the law of your state holds *both* spouses liable for the legitimate family expenses of *either*. For example, if you have signed up for a credit card such as Master Charge or Visa, and if your spouse is an authorized signatory on the account, then you will both be liable for any charges as a matter of contract obligation. If your spouse is charging necessities such as food and clothing, even if it is with merchants with whom you have never dealt, you may still be jointly liable under family-expense laws. These laws vary from state to state, and a lawyer should be consulted to see, for example, whether you can be held liable for the mink coat your wife has charged or the expensive boat your husband has contracted to buy—as distinct from clothing for the children. In some states it is a defense to such charges that you are living separate and apart without your fault. In most cases these accounts will have to be settled as part of an overall settlement or court adjudication.

The disposition of these bills could be a key stumbling block in resolving a case. As a general rule, if charges are made out of necessity and not in violation of a court injunction, the supporting spouse will usually pay them as a matter of course. But if charges are made for unnecessary items or out of vindictiveness, the other spouse may refuse to pay them, and final settlement is stymied until someone agrees to assume liability.

79. Should I establish my own credit?

It is wise to do this under any circumstances. Although creditors may be willing to add an unemployed spouse to a credit account while the parties are living together as husband and wife, the unemployed spouse may have difficulty when a separation or divorce is discovered. In spite of recent federal credit legislation, most creditors are still hesitant to extend credit to someone who has no visible means of support. Therefore, it makes sense before any formal dissolution proceedings to write a creditor and obtain cards in your individual name if you don't already have them. See the Credit Guide on page 46 for information on applying for credit.

80. How should I apply for credit if my husband and I had accounts together?

First, be sure to list your *best* credit accounts. Tell the creditor about accounts you shared with your husband. The creditor must consider this credit history when evaluating your application if you can show it applies to you. If the accounts are not on file at your local credit bureau, the creditor should call the previous creditors to verify the information you provided.

81. If the credit history from my marriage is bad, and I'm not responsible for it, what can I do?

Give a creditor information which shows that this history should not be used against you. This would be true, for example, if the wife signed her husband's application for a card he used only for business. She never saw the bills and didn't know of the account's delinquent status. A creditor may take this into consideration when evaluating her application for an individual account.

On the other hand, if a department-store account is in the husband's name, but is used primarily by the wife, and the account has been delinquent, this also needs to be called to the attention of the creditor.

82. What do I do if I am denied credit?

Make sure you ask the creditor why. Under the Equal Credit Opportunity Act (ECOA), you have the right to know the specific reasons your application was denied. If you ask to see your file within thirty days after you are notified that your credit application was denied, the bureau cannot charge you a fee for disclosure.

Next, check the report for accuracy and act on any misrepresentations. Then try to give the creditor any additional information that will show that you are a good credit risk.

Unfortunately, the financial irresponsibility of your spouse may have an adverse effect on your good credit rating. Credit organizations in your area will pick up the poor payment records of either spouse and attribute them to both husband and wife. The only way out of this problem is to ask particular retailers what credit services they are using and then apply to *each* service for correction of the records regarding you personally. While the appeal process may vary with each credit service, persistence in applying to a responsible officer with a detailed explanation of who was liable for the credit abuse should expunge the bad record.

83. What do we do about credit cards during and after divorce?

"During" refers to questions 77 and 78. At the end of a divorce the cards should be in the name of only one spouse to absolve the other of financial responsibility and to protect the continuing credit history of that card. If one spouse takes the card as part of the divorce settlement, the other spouse should inform the creditor that he or she is no longer responsible for that account.

For more information about your right to a separate credit history write:

44

Credit History
Division of Credit Practices
Federal Trade Commission
Washington, D.C. 20580

See the Credit Guide on page 46.

84. Should I file a joint income-tax return with my spouse?

In most cases the answer is yes, if a joint return saves you both money. A joint return *cannot* be filed for the year in which you are divorced, but often there is an overlap, and part of a settlement agreement will involve tax returns and division of tax refunds or liability. If an arbitrary refusal to sign a joint return results in a substantial financial loss, that loss will usually be reflected in some other aspect of the settlement by a disproportionate division of property or an increase or reduction of support. Your attorney will encourage you to file a joint return if it is to your mutual benefit.

If the taxable income comes primarily from your spouse and you fear the information provided the Internal Revenue Service will not be legitimate, insist on a written indemnification from your spouse for liability for additional taxes or penalties. Even if you did not prepare the return or make misrepresentations regarding your personal income or deductions, Internal Revenue will seek collection from both of you, but the indemnification will entitle you to reimbursement from your spouse for any loss.

CONSIDER: If the difference between a joint and an individual return is substantial, the willingness to file jointly can be an important leverage factor in settlement negotiations.

85. How can I find hidden assets?

By meticulously checking and tracing facts surrounding the acquisition and disposition of marital assets. Your present knowledge and the Check List on page 49 will get you started. Discuss your search and your discoveries with your lawyer, but *not* with your spouse. The more information you can find without your spouse's knowing that you are looking, the less likelihood of covering up. Your spouse is more likely to be caught in lies or evasions if you keep what you have found out about hidden assets to yourself and your lawyer. Breast-your-cards is the rule where gamesmanship is in operation. (See Chapter X for Discovery Procedures.)

CONSIDER: Don't confront your spouse with proven lies without leveraging that knowledge to your advantage in future negotiations or litigation. *Don't waste it on a self-righteous scene.*

CREDIT GUIDE

What is a credit history?

A record of your payments on credit cards, charge accounts, installment loans, and mortgages.

Why do I need a good credit history?

Many people, especially women, are denied credit each year because they can't prove they handled credit well before. A good credit history will assure future credit success.

How do creditors find out about my credit history?

They ask you questions about your credit accounts or references on their application forms. Creditors may also ask for reports from credit bureaus. These reports confirm the references you provide and give a full picture of your financial situation.

What is a credit bureau?

A company that gathers and sells credit information about consumers. The bureau sends the creditor whatever information is on file about you. It will report how many and what kinds of credit accounts you have, how you pay your bills, and whether you have ever filed for bankruptcy or been sued for payment.

Where does the credit bureau get its information?

Directly from the creditors. The only accounts which will appear in the files are those which make *regular* reports to the bureaus. While most national credit-card companies report their accounts to the bureau, many local creditors do not. In addition, some creditors only report accounts which are delinquent and fail to report accounts with a good payment history.

Suppose creditors didn't have or didn't furnish information on me?

Then the credit bureau will report that it has "no file" on you. "No file" reports can cause an application to be rejected.

What if all our credit accounts were listed only under my spouse's name?

You may have problems. Many women who had the responsibility of paying monthly bills on time discover after being widowed or divorced that their credit history is all in their husband's name. Creditors may get a "no file" report from the credit bureau.

A woman who marries and changes her name can have the same problem. The old accounts held in her maiden name may not be transferred to the file listed under her married name and her credit history may get lost. When applying for credit, mention your maiden name if you used it fairly recently.

What do I do if I never had credit?

Start building a good record now. A local bank or a drugstore or department store will often approve your credit application even if you don't meet the standards of a national creditor. It is a way to begin, and these people will become your future references.

Can I apply for as many accounts as I want?

No. Don't apply for too many accounts at one time. Credit bureaus keep a record of each creditor who inquires about you. Some creditors will deny your application if they think that you are opening too many new accounts in a short period of time. *Remember:* Most creditors are in business to *grant* credit, not deny it.

What if I shared accounts with my spouse which were established before June 1, 1977, and now are closed?

Under the ECOA the creditor must report information on shared accounts established *after* June 1, 1977, to bureaus in both spouses' names. However, to check on prior accounts, visit or phone your local credit bureau to check whether these accounts are in your file. They are still a part of your credit history even though they are closed. If these accounts were reported only in your husband's or former husband's name, ask to have them added to your file too. The credit bureau cannot charge you a fee for placing information already reported under your husband's name into a file accessible under your name.

Even if the accounts aren't in your husband's file, ask the bureau to add them to your file. You may need to pay a fee for each item added.

How about accounts opened after June 1, 1977?

In such accounts, you must indicate on the application whether you want to share the account with your spouse. Again, the creditor must report information on shared accounts established after June 1, 1977, to credit bureaus in both spouses' names.

How can I have credit information on accounts opened before June 1, 1977, included in my file?

Fill out the following form (make copies for the number of forms you will need) and send it to the creditor you wish to report your history to the bureau. This will be useful if particular applications are denied or ignored.

CREDIT HISTORY FOR MARRIED PERSONS

Send a copy of this form to your *creditors* to have credit history information on existing accounts which were opened *before* June 1, 1977, reported to credit bureaus in both spouses' names.

Under the Equal Credit Opportunity Act, I request that you report all credit information on this account in both our names.

_____

Account number

Name—Print or Type

_____
First   *Middle*   *Last*

_____
First   *Middle*   *Last*

_____
Street, Number, Apt.

_____
City, State, Zip

_____

Signature of either spouse

48

HIDDEN ASSET CHECK LIST

In the course of discovery, most spouses believe that their counterpart has somehow hidden or failed to disclose the existence of certain assets. (See Chapter X, Discovery Procedures.) The following check list may assist you in determining the whereabouts of hidden assets or whether in fact they exist.

1. Financial statements: Any loans made by your spouse from lending institutions in prior years require the filling out of sworn financial statements. In most cases, the borrower is trying to impress the lending institution with the extent of assets and may "puff" or overstate the case. In any event, looking back five years or so at these statements may put you on the trail of assets which are at present unaccounted for or which show valuations of assets substantially greater than what is now claimed.

2. Personal income-tax returns: A review of the personal returns filed by your spouse during the past five years may indicate sources of interest or dividends you didn't know about. You can then trace the disposition of the savings accounts or stocks up to the present time. The returns may also reveal unknown sources of income or loss from trusts, partnerships, or real estate holdings.

3. Corporate tax returns: If your spouse is the principal owner of a closely held corporation, he may be manipulating his salary by taking loans from the corporation or charging personal expenses to corporate accounts which will later be reimbursed or charged to the officer's loan account. Corporate returns should also be checked for excessive or unnecessary retained earnings (undistributed profits) which may disguise available profit distributions or an artificially low salary level. Reimbursement of prior capital contributions or repayment of loans to the corporation may also provide hidden cash flow to your spouse.

4. Partnership returns: The comparison of your spouse's partnership returns (IRS Forms 1065 and K1) over the years when the returns are available will indicate any sudden changes in his or her partnership interest or distribution. Such changes often occur at the time of a divorce and then compensating adjustments are made after the divorce is completed. Partners are sometimes willing to agree to such arrangements in order to keep you from breaking up or in some manner interfering with the partnership. If business expenses are charged to the partnership, you will want to know the extent of your spouse's charges as compared to those of the other partners. The same is true of reimbursed expenses.

5. Canceled checks and check registers from personal, partnership

Hidden Asset Check List, continued.

and closed corporation accounts: While time-consuming, it is always revealing to check over *all* the canceled checks and bank statements from personal accounts for the past few years, posting the expenditures to different columns under utilities, entertainment, loan payments, and so on. You will learn the amount of your total expenditures per year, which sometimes exceeds income, and you will have a better feeling for cost of living and where budget cuts should be made. In terms of hidden assets, you may come across canceled checks for expenditures for the purchase or maintenance of property which you never knew existed. It is important to check the canceled checks off against the appropriate bank statement to make sure that you have *all* of the canceled checks. It is possible that certain checks were removed before they were delivered to you. If your spouse writes checks on a partnership or corporate account where expenditures for the purchase or maintenance of property could be hidden, it is a good idea to check these canceled checks and bank statements as well. You may also uncover expenditures for your spouse's personal benefit which are given a false business posting on the corporation books or income-tax returns.

6. Savings-account passbooks: Acquire the passbooks for any savings accounts in which your spouse has had an interest during the past five years or more. Look for any deposits or withdrawals that are unusual in amount, or in pattern. A monthly withdrawal or deposit of money in the same odd amount may reflect mortgage payments or income receipts from sources that you are not aware of. Any such deposits or withdrawals will have to be explained as to source or purpose.

7. Securities or commodities account statements: If your spouse has been buying and selling stocks or bonds or dealing in commodities, the broker with whom he or she trades furnishes monthly or quarterly statements indicating all transactions. A review of these statements going back a few years could reveal the existence of securities of which you had no knowledge or could raise questions as to the disposition of stock sale proceeds. Cross-checking securities transactions and bank accounts by date and amount will usually verify the source or disposition of the monies involved. If the securities are sold and the proceeds unaccounted for, you can be sure the money's out there somewhere.

8. Expense-account abuse: Very often a corporate employer will allow its employees a great deal of leeway in their expense-account reporting. Your spouse may take advantage of this by exaggerating or even falsifying business expenditures. The employer maintains records as to expense-account disbursements to your spouse over the year with monthly detail. A check of these records will indicate the extent to which your spouse is able to "live off" the expense account and whether there are charges made for dinners in Los Angeles during periods when you know your spouse was home in Cleveland. A cross-check between corporate expense-account disbursements and savings- or checking-account deposits may indicate a pattern of expense-account abuse if the deposits exceed legitimate business expenditures.

9. Deferred salary increase, uncollected bonus or commissions: It is always a good idea to check directly by subpoena or otherwise with your spouse's employer to determine whether a salary increase is overdue, when it will be forthcoming, and how much it is. Employers are sometimes sympathetic to their divorcing employees and willing to bend the rules slightly to defer salary increases, bonuses, or commissions in order to suppress apparent income. Ultimately, these increases, bonuses, or commissions must be paid to keep the corporate books straight, and the employer will rarely lie when put under oath or forced to make a written statement on the subject. Sympathy goes just so far.

10. Safe-deposit–box activity: The bank that maintains your safe-deposit box keeps records of who enters the box and when. These records will not indicate contents of a box or what, if anything, has been removed. If you were aware of the contents at the point when the records indicate your spouse opened the box and something is now missing, you have a pretty good idea of who took it.

11. Cash transaction and in-kind compensation: Your spouse may be a physician or a shopkeeper, or in some other work where cash is paid, or he or she may receive in-kind compensation, where something of value other than cash is given in exchange for services. Such cash payments or noncash items are rarely reported on income-tax returns, but if you know of such income in the past and can subpoena current information, it will help in proving available income in excess of that shown on the income-tax returns. If your spouse buys things of substantial value with cash, there is probably a source of cash income somewhere. Most people don't retain cash in a noninterest-bearing form unless they're hiding its source.

12. Children's bank accounts: Frequently, a spouse who wishes to hide money will open a custodial account in the name of a child. Deposits and withdrawals are made without any intent that the child have use of the account except in case of the spouse's death. The interest from these accounts is not shown on income-tax returns, nor are returns filed for the children. A trace on the source and disposition of these accounts may lead you to other assets.

Hidden Asset Check List, continued.

13. Personal knowledge of spouse's habits: One of the most useful discovery tools is your personal knowledge of your spouse's habits with money. Very seldom will people who are attempting to hide money do so without making some form of written note. When things are going well in a marriage, your spouse may tell you about such records, but you can be sure they will disappear in case of divorce. Look for them in the typical hiding places around the home or office. Make photostats without your spouse's knowledge, if possible. The more secretive a person is, the more detailed such notes are likely to be. If your spouse has neglected to declare income to Internal Revenue Service, your knowledge of hidden income or assets may prove to be a powerful leverage factor in reaching a satisfactory settlement.

14. Phony income-tax returns: When the divorce has been filed, some spouses are inclined to alter the *copies* of their previously filed income-tax returns in order to hide or adjust pertinent financial information. If you have reason to believe that copies furnished you or your lawyer have been altered, ask for copies of jointly filed returns directly from Internal Revenue Service. If you are not a signatory to the return, your spouse can be asked to execute the request form. If he or she refuses, you have reason to believe that your suspicions are accurate.

15. Phony loans or debts: In order to keep cash from being divided, a spouse may sometimes attempt to bury the money with a phony loan to a cooperative friend or relative. The loan may be tied up with a long-term note or with a claimed likelihood of uncollectibility, so as to remove this money from consideration at settlement time. By having your lawyer question the alleged borrower under oath, you may find that the loan was either never made or was made on the understanding that the money involved would be immediately returned upon request. Using basically the same technique, your spouse may claim a debt to a friend or a relative which must be paid before any division of marital property is made. For example, when a loan is made by a parent or grandparent for the down payment on a house, it is more often than not a gift, with no expectation of repayment. A tip-off to this situation is that only the spouse claiming the debt has signed a note to the relative. The other spouse, who was never aware of the debt or who understood it to be a gift, of course did not sign the note because it probably came into existence *after* the divorce proceedings commenced. Sudden payment of debts to out-of-state creditors who are not available for deposition is usually a sign that the debt is a phony.

16. "Friend" or other phonies on the payroll: If your spouse is in a position to control the payroll of a sole proprietorship, partnership, or closely held corporation, he may be paying salaries to a friend or relative who is not actually providing services commensurate with the compensation. The friend on the payroll may be stashing the money away for your spouse or they may be both enjoying it currently. In either case, the profit of the enterprise will be reduced accordingly and your spouse may be drawing a lesser salary. The same ploy can be used for payment to phony independent contractors.

17. Retirement-plan abuse: If your spouse has established a pension or profit-sharing plan in connection with a closely held corporation, the plan should be carefully checked to determine whether monies that have been contributed to the account are being invested in accordance with the plan requirements. Very often, deductions will be taken for contributions to such plans, and then the monies are used for personal living expenses or taken out as loans which are never repaid. While Internal Revenue Service does impose severe penalties if such pension abuse is discovered, still these plans do provide an opportunity to secrete assets unless they are closely monitored.

18. Defined benefit pension plans: Defined-benefit pension plans are distinguished from defined-contribution plans by the fact that the benefits payable at retirement age are specified within the plan itself rather than by some contribution formula. The amount of the contributions then must be actuarially determined, based on the age of the intended beneficiary and the point at which benefits are to be paid. A great deal of income can be buried by substantial payments into such a plan during the years preceding or during divorce litigation. The required payments can be a substantial portion of the beneficiary's income, if that is what is required to achieve the defined goal at retirement. This, of course, leaves little money available for support or division as marital property. Once the divorce is completed, the defined-benefit plan can be discarded, even though a substantial tax loss may result.

19. Gift and inheritance tax returns: Much useful information is available from inheritance, estate, or gift-tax returns of relatives you believe have been generous to your spouse. If these returns show that there were substantial gifts or bequests that have not been accounted for in the settlement negotiations, you are alerted that other assets could also be hidden. A tracing will have to be made from the estate's distribution to see what has happened to the assets.

YOU AND YOUR LAWYER

86. Should I tell my lawyer the whole truth?

Yes. A relationship of trust and credibility is a must between you and your lawyer, and he has the same obligation to tell you the truth. If you lie about assets or income or other facts, his credibility will be undermined when he deals with your spouse's lawyer, because at some point the facts are likely to come out. If your lawyer suggests that you should lie or tacitly approves misrepresentations, you probably have the wrong lawyer. A competent lawyer does not become enmeshed in the gamesmanship of battling spouses. To the extent that he does, his effectiveness is reduced.

In almost every case your spouse will know when you're lying, even if it can't be proved. The natural reaction to such deception will be counter-measures that are sure to escalate the subterfuge, animosity, and expense. In other words, *you* will be the loser. Make it your rule from the outset to present your lawyer with *all the facts*, and then let him worry about protecting your best interests in connection with those facts. He can't anticipate and plan around pitfalls he's not aware of. Also, a lawyer can make reasonably

54

accurate predictions about the outcome of your case only if you give him accurate information to work with.

87. When should I telephone my lawyer?

Your lawyer probably cannot guarantee a time when he will be in his office and available for calls. Many lawyers have to go to court almost every morning and they have to review files or confer with clients beforehand. Therefore, avoid calls between 9 and 10 A.M. By the same token, do not call after 5 P.M. or at the lawyer's home unless it is an emergency which *must* be dealt with immediately. Most questions have to wait until the next morning before they can be acted upon anyway.

Ask your lawyer if there is a particular time he will be available for calls—or can return calls. (Some lawyers do return calls in the evening after a hectic day. Others will schedule your return calls if they are frequently out of the office.)

Leave a message with the lawyer's secretary and if possible explain the reason you are calling. The secretary may have the information that you are seeking or be able to get it for you. If so, you can save yourself time and money, because your lawyer working on an hourly fee basis will bill for your call, while his secretary may not. Busy lawyers usually hire secretaries who are really legal assistants capable of dealing with many of your problems.

CAUTION: If your use of the telephone becomes a source of irritation to the lawyer, he or she will simply avoid that irritation by not returning your calls. Sometimes such an attitude is justified —sometimes it is cause for questioning whether you are receiving the service you need. (See Question 89.)

88. How is my lawyer's secretary important to me?

The secretary is probably aware of your case and of the correspondence and telephone calls between your lawyer and your spouse's lawyer. Although he or she may not be able to discuss the content of these communications, he or she can reassure you that they took place. Whenever possible, use the secretary (or paralegal if the lawyer has one) for information about calendar dates, court times, depositions, and office appointments. Limit contact with your lawyer to more important matters.

If the secretary finds you easy and reasonable to deal with, your case will get priority. In a well-organized law office the secretary has substantial authority in scheduling appointments, depositions, court dates, and the like. The difficult clients may get poorer service because office personnel avoid them. The lawyer often has time to return only those calls selected by the secretary on a priority basis. Put yourself on the priority list by establishing a positive relationship with the lawyer's secretary.

89. What if my lawyer doesn't return my telephone calls?

The telephone is one of the principal areas of irritation between lawyers and clients in matrimonial cases. The lawyer who regularly fails to return calls and the client who calls daily or at the lawyer's home are equally at fault.

Remember, although this is the only divorce case you have, your lawyer has many more. Do not telephone your attorney to ventilate personal frustration over your broken marriage or the progress of your divorce. Use the phone to exchange necessary information. Handle longer communications by letter or office visit. You have every right to expect your calls to be returned, if not the same day, at least the day after. Begin recording all your telephone calls, indicating the date and the time of the call. If you see a series of logged calls which have not been returned, ask yourself if you have misused the telephone. If so, the lawyer is probably avoiding you. If not, a polite letter outlining the occasions when your calls were not returned will bring your dissatisfaction to your lawyer's attention, and probably earn you special attention.

You will appreciate the lawyer's economical use of the telephone when you're in the office and no outside calls are accepted. Nothing is more irritating than sitting in a lawyer's office and listening to him deal with other cases. If he fills out little pink time slips, every time *your* appointment is interrupted by a call, remind him to deduct fifteen minutes from your bill for each one.

90. Can I call my spouse's lawyer if my lawyer is out of town?

No. And if the lawyer calls your spouse at home and you happen to answer the phone, do not engage in conversation about *any* aspect of the case.

91. What if my lawyer doesn't answer my questions?

He or she may have, but perhaps you didn't understand the answer or have forgotten it. These are emotional times, so it is understandable if this occurs. Always prepare and write down specific questions before you meet with or call your lawyer. Once you arrive at the office you may forget many of the questions that were going through your mind at two or three o'clock the previous morning. A lawyer always appreciates the client who prepares a list or agenda for any conference or telephone conversation. There is much less drifting as a result, and you come away feeling satisfied that all questions have been covered.

If an answer to a particular question is not satisfactory or you do not understand the answer, tell your lawyer so immediately. *Don't be afraid to show your lack of understanding.* Your lawyer wants to know when you do not understand aspects of the case. He or she is paid to know the answers to your questions and to explain them thoroughly, but you must ask the right questions.

CAUTION: People under stress are usually poor listeners. When you ask your lawyer a question, *listen to the answers* rather than thinking ahead to your next question. Don't be afraid to take notes. Again, if you brought a list of questions, you don't have to think ahead to your next one.

92. Does the lawyer ever sell out his client for a bigger fee?

Everyone seems to think so at one point or another. The reason for this is not a lot of dishonest lawyers but that a good matrimonial lawyer does not simply do what the client *wants* him or her to do. The lawyer is paid by you for special knowledge and professional judgment. Exercising that judgment in your best interests often means *opposing* you. The fact that your lawyer does not share your animosity toward your spouse or your spouse's lawyer doesn't mean he or she is part of a conspiracy to sell you down the river.

It is not unusual for a litigant to see the issues in black and white. Your lawyer has an obligation to dispel this attitude, to advise you on the strong points of your spouse's case and the weak points of your own. You should appreciate straight advice because people under stress are prone to self-deception. Those lawyers who claim to be representing "the good guy" in every case rarely settle their cases. Their own self-righteousness fuels their client's emotionalism and misconceptions. They won't compromise because their goals are unrealistic. The result may be an expensive and time-consuming trial before a judge who is likely to be put off by such attitudes anyhow.

An effective lawyer will discourage his own client's arbitrary or vindictive demands, and expects the same "client control" from opposing counsel. In that way the potential for amicable settlement or even reconciliation is far greater. This natural difference between a forceful lawyer and an emotional client sometimes leads to unjustified questions as to the lawyer's loyalty.

93. What if I don't agree with my lawyer in the matter of strategy or tactics?

You should tell your lawyer immediately and give him or her an opportunity to explain why a particular course should be followed. Although you hired the lawyer for his expertise, you should also explain your opposition to a particular course, because you are the ultimate decision-maker. You pay the bills.

A lawyer is justified in refusing to follow a course of action that he feels is unethical or contrary to your best interests. For example, if you feel your children should be called as witnesses to testify on some issue of misconduct by your spouse, and your lawyer resists calling them, discuss this matter with him. You should be willing to trust your lawyer in matters of strategy and tactics because that is why you hired him. But if you've lost faith in him, or if you can't agree on a point of dispute, consider getting a second legal opinion or hiring a new lawyer.

94. Can I fire my lawyer?

Absolutely. You can hire and fire all the lawyers you can afford to pay. However, if a client has fired more than two or three lawyers, there is probably more wrong with the client than with the lawyers.

If you want to fire your present lawyer, it is advisable to have the next lawyer available to substitute immediately. Hiring multiple lawyers is generally an indication of a controversial contested case, and you should not be left representing yourself for any interim period. Very often, the second lawyer will refuse to become involved in the case until the reasonable fee demands of the first lawyer have been met or arrangements made for payment. In most states the withdrawing lawyer cannot refuse to deliver the contents of your file to the new lawyer, but he may be entitled to go before the court to seek an award of fees and costs advanced on your behalf.

If you don't want to fire your first lawyer but want to bring in a second lawyer for additional expertise, both lawyers can remain in the case and cooperate in your representation. If this procedure is followed, you should have an understanding between the lawyers as to whether or not you will be charged by both of them.

95. Can I get a second legal opinion without firing my lawyer?

Yes. Just go to another lawyer you have reason to believe is competent in the matrimonial field. Tell him the facts as accurately as you can and ask his opinion. Don't be afraid to disclose your present lawyer's advice. The new lawyer should be given all the information he needs to be able to evaluate your presentation of the facts.

While most lawyers don't enjoy second-guessing, the new counsel should be willing to confirm whether the first opinion is reasonable or not. He may even be able to suggest new alternatives, and awareness of alternatives is a prerequisite to good decision-making. Your first lawyer may not have explained certain alternatives because he presumed they would be unacceptable to you.

CONSIDER: If you find that you are regularly questioning your lawyer's opinion on matters of professional judgment, he is probably not for you, and a new lawyer should be sought. You should have as much faith in your divorce lawyer as you would in your brain surgeon.

96. Can I object to the amount of fees charged by my lawyer?

Of course, and you *should* complain if the fees are unreasonable. Complain directly to the lawyer if the amount charged is contrary to your understanding with him. If he refuses to or cannot give a reasonable explanation for his fee, you can refuse to pay, forcing him to sue you. The court then determines what the proper fees are and takes into account any valid fee agreement existing between you. Contrary to popular belief, you will have no problem finding a lawyer to represent you over a legitimate fee dispute, and courts lean more toward clients than lawyers in these cases.

Your local bar association probably has a grievance procedure whereby they review fee complaints and sometimes even conduct hearings or arbitrations between the lawyer and client. If the lawyer fails to cooperate in those proceedings and the client appears to have a legitimate complaint, the matter is forwarded to the state disciplinary body. They will consider sanctions against the lawyer.

Divorce is such an emotional undertaking that bad feelings or misunderstandings can arise even between clients and their own lawyers, and, most especially, when the question of fees arises. In almost every instance, it is best to work out any disagreement informally with your lawyer. He wants to avoid litigation or bar-association inquiries, and you want to avoid paying a lawyer to defend a suit for fees by your previous lawyer—thereby incurring more fees.

97. Is it all right to date or have a sexual relationship with my lawyer?

A recent ethics opinion in the State of Oregon has held that it is not improper for an attorney to have a sexual relationship with his client in a divorce case if children are not involved or as long as the outcome of the case is not affected.

Most people would be appalled at that opinion, and in fact *any* personal relationship between attorney and client is bound to undermine the attorney's objectivity to some degree. The quality of your representation is likely to be adversely affected as a result. Clients are especially vulnerable at this juncture in their life, and in most cases it would be unfair for the attorney to take advantage of someone who is emotionally insecure. On the other hand, some emotionally vulnerable clients seem to want their attorney's personal attentions and encourage special treatment beyond the call of legal representation. In any event, a personal relationship between attorney and client should be discouraged. If the attraction remains after the case is resolved, the parties are free to do as they please.

THE CASE BEGINS

98. How does a case start?

Usually with the filing of the Complaint for Divorce or Legal Separation. The Complaint and a Summons are then served upon the other party by the sheriff. Without the service of Summons, the court lacks jurisdiction over the other party and cannot order various things to be done, such as the payment of support. If a written appearance is filed voluntarily on behalf of the defendant, personal jurisdiction is achieved and a Summons need not be served.

99. Does it matter who files for the divorce?

In most cases, no. The amount of property and support awards is not affected by whether the plaintiff is the husband or wife. From a leverage standpoint, however, the party who most wants the divorce is likely to give up something during negotiations to get the case over with faster. You may gain some strategic advantage by allowing the other side to file, if you are in no particular hurry.

100. What if my spouse avoids service of summons?

If your spouse cannot be found by the sheriff within your state for purposes of serving Summons, the court can still grant the divorce. Notice of filing your Complaint must be published in a local newspaper and a statutory period of time must pass (usually thirty days) to give the other party an opportunity to respond. This is what is commonly called a publication or *default* divorce. The only relief the court can grant by its decree is the divorce itself and custody of children living with you. The court cannot award alimony or child support until the missing spouse is found. If your spouse has property within the state, the court can assume jurisdiction over the property to satisfy support needs.

101. Is it all right to discuss the divorce with my spouse?

Your lawyer would prefer that you do not discuss matters involving property or support or matters to be negotiated later. If you are in a fault state, you certainly do not want to discuss grounds with your spouse. The only areas left, therefore, are matters of reconciliation or dealing with the children. The details of the case itself should not be discussed unless your lawyer approves. What you say to your spouse may compromise your negotiating position and may have to be *un-said* by the lawyer in the negotiating process. When you offer $100 in a casual conversation with your spouse, and your attorney intended to offer $70, you may end up paying $125. You just gave the opposition "openers."

Sometimes your lawyer may want to pass along certain information to your spouse through you. Strategically you can affect the negotiations by conveying ideas to your spouse that will get back to the opposing lawyer and influence his perceptions of negotiation priorities. Hints that your job is in jeopardy or that you're being transferred to another state can be conveyed, for example, to make the other side anxious to settle now. When lawyer communications break down you may want to call your spouse to get things started again. Such strategy should *only* be used under the instruction of your lawyer.

102. Can I discuss my case with friends and relatives?

It would be extraordinary if you didn't. You need to ventilate your fears and frustrations during this difficult period.

CAUTION: The confidant who is a gossip or informant to your spouse can ruin your case. So can you, if you talk too much.

103. What is an uncontested case?

It is any suit for divorce, legal separation, or annulment in which the final judgment is entered *without the necessity of a trial.*

The majority of cases start out to be contested, at least on certain issues. Usually, though, these issues are resolved, and a written agreement is drawn and presented to the court for approval. Thus a contested case has become uncontested (agreed).

The final court hearing required to prove the grounds for divorce and to present the agreement to the judge for approval is not really a trial because everything has already been agreed. When the judge signs the decree of divorce containing the agreement, the case is completed.

104. At what point does my case become contested?

Your case is contested from the moment it is filed until a settlement has been reached. "Contested" simply means that some issues relating to the divorce—custody, property, or support—have not been resolved.

Sometimes there is a contested trial because of a dispute about matters of fact or law which must be submitted to the judge for determination. Other cases go to trial because one or both of the parties are either bluffing or arbitrary in their demands.

105. What is involved in a contested case?

A contested case consists of written pleadings, temporary motions, discovery procedures, settlement negotiations, pretrial hearings and finally, if all else fails, the trial and judgment of the court. These terms are defined in the Glossary.

REMEMBER: Since every case is contested until the issues are resolved, you proceed as if your case were going to trial until an agreement is reached. The procedures for discovery, negotiation, and temporary motions are essentially the same in all cases. It is the level of cooperation that controls the informality and speed of the proceedings.

106. Is an uncontested case cheaper?

Definitely. Even the simplest case that is agreed at the outset takes from six to ten hours to process, from initial interview to final decree. The variation in charges for such a case is based primarily on the lawyer's time spent advising the clients, suggesting alternatives, and drafting the agreement and decree. If simple forms are used, and most work is done by a paralegal, the cost will be minimal. Most legal clinics handle a divorce case this way. If a case has contested issues and more lawyer's time is required, the cost will increase accordingly.

Even if a case is *substantially* agreed, the fees will be higher in a case requiring the skills of the lawyer as a negotiator or tax planner. Although the amount of property transferred and support paid will affect the amount of the fees, contingency fee arrangements (where lawyers get a percentage of the settlement) are forbidden for divorce cases in most states.

107. Are there any advantages other than cost in working out a settlement?

Yes. There are several. First, the negotiated settlement will more likely accommodate *your* needs and desires. When your lawyer bargains over particular issues he keeps your priorities in mind, just as the opposing lawyer does for his client. Good negotiators are aware of these priorities and accommodate those which are not in conflict. Those that *are* in conflict must be traded and compromised until the final bargain is reached.

In most cases that come to trial, the judge does not know these priorities because both sides are asking for everything and hoping to get as much as possible. For example, certain items of property will have special intrinsic value to one of the spouses, but the court may have no knowledge of this fact in making its division. The trial judge may believe he is giving the wife the better deal by awarding her the main residence and awarding the summer cottage to the husband. But if she has a strong sentimental attachment to the summer home and really has no desire to live in the marital residence, the result is a loss to her. Only through negotiation can the parties accommodate their particular priorities, many of which may have little connection with dollar values.

The second advantage in negotiated settlement is that the lawyers can be more creative in tailoring the settlement agreement to the mutual benefit of the parties. For example, child support and alimony can be paid on an unallocated basis in order that they be fully taxable to the wife and fully deductible to the husband. This can result in a substantial tax savings if the wife has less income than the husband. The tax burden is then shared between the parties at a much lower rate, and the whole family benefits. If the award is left up to the court, there is more likely to be an allocation between alimony and child support, and the Internal Revenue Service will reap the benefits to the detriment of the family. Rarely does a trial judge have the time and sometimes not even

64

the expertise to project the tax results of the settlement which he orders.

Court-ordered judgments may not be as thorough as carefully drafted settlement agreements, because the lawyers are more or less bound by the findings of the court in drafting the divorce decree. A Settlement Considerations Check List appears on page 86. Trial judges rarely use such a check list and therefore fail to rule on many of the provisions that could have been added to a negotiated settlement agreement.

Another advantage in negotiating your settlement is the likelihood of greater cooperation in carrying out the terms. Compromise, although painful, more often leads to compliance with the terms because both parties participated in the result. A court decision forced on the parties may leave one or both disgruntled and inclined to resist carrying out the provisions they disliked.

108. What are the pleadings?

They are the papers you file to formally put your case before the court. They tell the judge what relief you want and why.

The initial pleading is usually the Complaint for Divorce (or Petition for Dissolution of Marriage, as it is called in many jurisdictions).

After being served with a Summons and Complaint, your spouse will file a pleading called an Answer (or Response), which either admits or denies the allegations contained in your Complaint.

If new factual matter is raised in the Answer, a Reply may be filed denying that new matter.

These are called the principal pleadings. Once these principal pleadings have been filed and discovery completed, the case is at issue and ready to be tried.

There are other pleadings called Petitions and Motions which ask for particular relief or raise technical objections to the principal pleading. For instance:

A Motion to Strike or Dismiss a Complaint or Petition may be filed because of some legal defect in the pleading.

A Petition to Show Cause may be filed claiming that one of the parties is in contempt of court for violation of some court order.

Other Petitions are filed seeking particular relief in connection with temporary support, custody, visitation, or injunctions.

Each pleading concludes with a "prayer" or paragraphs which specify the relief requested. Some states require that pleadings containing factual allegations be sworn to or supported by your sworn affidavit. In that case the response to the pleading must also be under oath.

109. What are orders, judgments, and decrees?

They are court rulings put in written form. An order is drafted as a result of a Petition or Motion for some specific relief and submitted to the court for signature. A Decree of Divorce or Judgment for Dissolution is simply a more detailed order which sets forth the final results of the divorce proceedings, whether by agreement or contested hearing. Orders, judgments, and decrees must be signed by the judge before they are appealable or enforceable.

110. What is a temporary motion?

It is a proceeding in which a party asks the court for some particular relief before the final judgment for divorce or legal separation. If the hearing requires testimony, the parties and supporting witnesses testify, and the court renders its judgment. A court order is then entered encompassing the details of the judge's ruling.

111. Do you have to give notice to the other side when you file a motion or petition?

Once the other side has filed an appearance or been served with Summons, advance notice must be given for any Motion or Petition, except in extreme emergencies or where irreparable injury is likely to result from the notice. *Both* sides must have an opportunity to be heard in court on any issues to be ruled upon by the judge.

112. What is an ex parte motion?

This occurs when no notice is given to the other side because you are seeking emergency relief or because you would suffer irreparable injury if advance notice were given. If, for example, you fear that assets will be hidden, your attorney can petition ex parte for a temporary restraining order forbidding the selling or secreting of those assets. The restraining order is then served on your spouse with a notice of hearing date when he or she will be given an opportunity to object to the order. If the assets are disposed of in the meantime, the court can then make the guilty party show cause why he or she should not be held in contempt for willful violation of the order.

A hearing is also ex parte if the other side is given notice but fails to appear.

113. Will I have to testify in connection with my temporary motion or petition?

If a factual issue is involved, someone with knowledge of the relevant facts will have to testify. For example, your testimony will be required to prove your need for temporary support, and your husband or wife will have to testify regarding his or her ability to pay. Failure to present convincing evidence by testimony (or affidavit in some states) will result in a denial of the petition. Failure to offer testimony or other convincing evidence in opposition to the petition will result in the requested relief being granted by default.

114. What information do I need when I apply for temporary alimony or child support?

This is the same information that you were gathering for your lawyer for the initial interview, strictly dollars-and-cents data relating to financial need and ability to pay. It is the practice in many courts to require you to prepare an affidavit detailing your fixed monthly living expenses, as well as all sources of income available to you and your spouse. Even if no affidavit is required, you should bring a list of your fixed living expenses (see page 162) to court and a copy of your latest cumulative pay-check stub. If that is not available, a letter from your employer detailing your gross income and itemized deductions will do. The court will also want a list of liquid assets such as savings and securities as these may have to be used if income is inadequate. (See the Asset/Liability Worksheet, page 157.)

115. Once a petition for temporary relief is filed, does the judge have to make the decision?

No, the relief requested can still be worked out by agreement of the parties or their lawyers. The petition was probably filed in the first place because the parties couldn't agree on a given point. However, once the parties are in court, the pressure of the anticipated hearing with its unpredictable result often produces an agreement before the actual hearing by the judge. In fact many temporary-motion judges *require* the lawyers to discuss matters in issue prior to hearing and to exchange any relevant discovery information, such as cost of living and the respective incomes of the parties. The temporary motion then becomes a form of discovery and provides a basis for the parties to reach a compromise temporary order.

REMEMBER: It is useful for the parties to learn to compromise at this early stage of the proceeding, because it sets the ground-work for an overall settlement later on.

116. Is there any advantage in reaching agreed orders in connection with temporary motions, as opposed to a decision made by the court?

Lawyers often prefer reaching temporary support arrangements by agreement to letting a judge rule. The judge typically has so many matters before him that he does not have time to grant a full hearing on the temporary issue. He is more likely to work by rule of thumb, written schedule, or some other time-saving device that might place an unfair burden on one of the parties. When the time gap between a temporary and final hearing is short, no great harm would be done but, in some jurisdictions, years can intervene between a temporary order and the final adjudication.

CAUTION: An inequitable temporary order can place such a burden on one of the parties that he or she is forced into a settlement at a distinct disadvantage. The beneficiary of the order also becomes harder to deal with.

117. What does "without prejudice" mean?

If you enter a temporary order "without prejudice," either party can seek a hearing to modify the order at a future time. Without that language you would have to prove a change in circumstances before the temporary order could be modified or terminated. For example, if you agree to pay $100 temporary child support per week without prejudice, you can later change your mind for *any* reason and obtain a hearing on the amount of support. The "without prejudice" order is binding, however, until terminated or until a new order is entered.

118. Do courts make temporary property divisions?

Almost never. *Use* of property, such as the marital home or an automobile, may be granted by the court on a temporary basis, but the actual award of property is usually reserved until after the judge has decided that there will be a decree for divorce.

119. Can the court order my spouse out of the house?

Yes, but most courts are reluctant to do that unless you can prove the likelihood of physical or serious psychological harm from remaining in the same household. The only alternatives are voluntary separation or "self-help." The latter means physically forcing someone off the premises or locking them out. Self-help is likely to have serious repercussions. Criminal charges can be brought for any physical force used, and changed locks often result in broken windows and doors and sometimes even bones.

When valid reason exists for physical separation, and a court order cannot be immediately obtained, it is probably best for the concerned spouse to leave voluntarily, pending court intervention. But, because leaving the home can have crucial strategic implications in your case, try to check with your lawyer before making the move. *If you are in danger, leave at once.*

120. How are temporary orders enforced?

If either party fails to comply with a provision of an order, a petition for contempt can be filed. The violator then will have to show reasonable cause for not complying or be punished by fine or imprisonment. He or she may also have pay checks and bank accounts garnisheed; and other property may be sold to satisfy unfulfilled financial obligations.

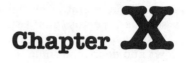

Chapter X

DISCOVERY PROCEDURES

121. How does my lawyer learn the facts about my case?

By following what are called discovery procedures.

Informal discovery begins with the initial interview with your lawyer. Your conversations, then and later, provide information about grounds, assets, expenses, and children. Your lawyer is also learning about *you* in the process—what your priorities are, the nature of your marital problems and what your plans are for after divorce. The documentation you provide expands this informal discovery procedure.

If your spouse is cooperating with you in the divorce, his lawyer adds to the informal discovery by *voluntarily* providing requested information and documentation.

Formal discovery involves legal procedures such as subpoenas, interrogatories, depositions, and notices to produce documents or things.

122. How does discovery begin?

You have already begun the Asset/Liability discovery process if you used the Hidden Asset Check List on page 49 and worksheet on p. 157 of this book, and brought the information to your lawyer. He may ask you to get more information, which may be available to you without requiring your spouse's cooperation. In the area of grounds, for instance, your friends and relatives may have information about your spouse's conduct when you were not present. Notice may also be served upon your spouse's lawyer, or a subpoena may be served upon individuals or institutions, like banks, which are not parties to the case, to provide certain information.

123. Do the lawyers ever do informal discovery?

Yes. In most cases the lawyers informally exchange information regarding their clients at the outset. The best lawyers do this without hesitation and give complete relevant financial facts. The lawyer knows he will be required to provide this information anyhow, and he can save time for you and himself, as well as the expense of formal discovery. Don't be surprised, then, if he *insists* that you voluntarily produce income-tax returns that you wanted to keep secret, or passbooks to savings accounts which your spouse may not know about.

Your lawyer expects to be voluntarily furnished with similar information by opposing counsel with the same degree of candor and completeness.

124. If I ask him to, will my lawyer refrain from giving complete and honest discovery?

Your lawyer is within his rights not to disclose information that is not requested, but he cannot go along with intentional deception. If your lawyer has a reputation among other lawyers for cooperation in these matters, you will benefit, and information will be exchanged inexpensively.

If you have a lawyer who joins you in concealing information, his reputation probably precedes him, and you can be sure that a substantial amount of *extra* time will be spent in expensive formal discovery procedures. If the opposing counsel *expects* deception, he will spend a lot more time looking for it.

125. Who is included in the discovery process?

Anybody who knows something that is relevant and important to your case. For example, depending on the issues, one or more of the following might be able to contribute necessary information:

Property division and support: Accountants, appraisers, actuaries, business associates, economists, bank personnel, past and present employers.

Child custody and grounds: Baby-sitters, housekeepers, people who have resided in your home, clergy, neighbors, psychological counselors or therapists, doctors, social-service investigators, friends or relatives, your spouse's former friends or lovers, private investigators, police.

126. Are there any benefits from the formal discovery procedures besides information?

Yes. Formal discovery establishes the factual record upon which your agreed settlement is based. In the event of any substantial misrepresentations, this record may be the basis for reconsidering a judgment when a fraud is discovered.

127. Can we settle our case without discovery?

Only if the financial and other facts on which the settlement is based are clear and undisputed. The simpler the case, the less discovery is needed and the more informal it is likely to be. Many cases are settled after a single conference between the parties and their lawyers, but cooperation with voluntary exchange of information is still required.

128. What is a deposition?

It is a statement, taken down in writing, that is your lawyer's primary formal discovery tool. There are two kinds of depositions. In the *evidence deposition*, the testimony is preserved for use at a later court hearing because the witness will not be available. Rules of evidence are strictly adhered to, just as at trial. When the deposition is completed, the testimony is transcribed by the court reporter, sealed in an envelope, and held by the court clerk to be read at the trial.

The *discovery deposition* is used primarily to discover information about issues that may arise in any later court proceeding. A discovery deposition also has a second important function: if you say one thing in the discovery deposition, and another thing at the trial, you will have to explain why your answer changed. The parts of the discovery deposition that are in conflict can be read to the witness at trial, and if the change is substantial and unexplained, the overall testimony of the witness is less believable.

129. What type of questions will they ask me at a discovery deposition?

If in your state marital misconduct is important in granting the divorce or awarding custody, property, or support, the lawyer will ask questions that relate to any alleged misbehavior. You will also be asked about income, assets, and financial need, as well as about the care and condition of the children if custody is an issue. A list of sample deposition questions is on the following page.

130. What do I have to bring with me to the deposition?

Only those books, records, and other documents requested by the other lawyer in his Notice of Deposition and approved by your lawyer. Where finances are at issue, you will typically be asked to bring such things as your bank records dating back two or three years, savings-account passbooks, deeds, wills, trust agreements, insurance policies, real estate closing statements, financial statements, and the like. If the notice requests documents that are not relevant or go beyond the bounds of reasonable discovery, the court can be petitioned for an order limiting discovery.

In most jurisdictions it is only necessary to bring those documents which are within your possession or accessible to you. You are not required to prepare documents which do not exist, such as a list of debts or a list of securities owned by you, but it is often a good idea to have such lists anyway. They will help you in the trial of your case and speed up the presentation of that information at the deposition. You can see that in getting ready for the discovery deposition you are actually beginning your preparation for a trial—just in case there is one.

CAUTION: Your failure to present *requested* documentation at the time of deposition may bar you from presenting that same documentation at the trial.

131. May I refuse to allow my spouse to be present when I give my deposition?

No, but other persons who are not parties to the deposition may be excluded. The parties themselves are entitled to be present at all court proceedings and depositions.

132. May I refuse to answer questions at a deposition?

Not unless your lawyer objects to the question and instructs you not to answer it. Remember that the purpose of the deposition is to provide information that will enable the other side to present its case or defend against yours. The questioner is given broad leeway in terms of relevancy to assure that his discovery will be complete. If, on the other hand, the same questions are being asked over and over, or the questioner is harassing you or has gone far beyond what is relevant, your lawyer may interpose objections

DEPOSITION QUESTIONS—SAMPLE

Grounds:

Where the subject matter of the deposition is grounds for divorce, some typical questions that may be asked are as follows:

PHYSICAL CRUELTY:

Did you strike your wife on or about April 10, 1979?

Did you have an argument with her at that time?

Who was present when you had the argument?

Did anyone witness the striking?

What part of your body came in contact with your wife's on this occasion?

What happened immediately following this incident?

Have there been other occasions when you and your wife have had physical altercations?

When?

Who was present?

What preceded the altercation?

Describe the altercation or striking.

What happened immediately following?

MENTAL CRUELTY:

What are examples of your husband's conduct toward you which you have characterized in your complaint as mental cruelty?

Did anyone witness this conduct? What are the names and addresses of people who have knowledge of this conduct?

ADULTERY:

I show you copies of your telephone calls, as furnished by the telephone company, for the months of January through June 1979 and ask you if you are the person who placed the calls to number 835-4059?

Who did you call at that number?

For what purpose?

Were you driving a 1979 gray Chevrolet automobile with license-plate number GN 4037 during the latter half of 1979?

Did you on any occasion park that automobile overnight in the driveway of a residence with a street address 215 South Green Street?

Did you ever spend the night at that residence?

Who else was present?

For what purpose was your automobile parked there?

Property and support

If the deposition is about alimony, child support, or property division, some typical questions might be:

INCOME:

How long have you worked at your present place of employment?

What deductions are taken from your pay check?

Have you ever received a bonus at that place of employment?

How many exemptions are you currently claiming for withholding purposes?

Have you in any manner altered your working hours since these divorce proceedings were commenced?

For what reason are you earning substantially less currently than you have earned over the preceding three years?

PROPERTY DIVISION:

Is anyone holding any money or property for you?

What was the source of the monies used for the down payment in purchasing your marital residence?

What contribution did your wife make in the operation of your business?

What are your outstanding personal debts and manner of repayment?

Have you incurred any debts since the commencement of these proceedings?

Do you have any debts involving personal friends or relatives?

Are those debts evidenced by promissory notes?

When were those notes drafted and signed?

When was the last time that you borrowed money from a banking institution?

Was a financial statement furnished by you in connection with that loan?

What have you done with the monies that you removed from the joint account you formerly maintained with the children?

What is your estimate of the current market value of the marital home?

Have you had the home appraised within the past twelve months?

What has been the trend of your business in terms of growth over the past five years?

What are your expectations for the coming years and on what factors do you principally base your predictions?

Deposition Questions, continued.

Alimony and child support

What are your personal fixed monthly living expenses?

What were you spending annually to maintain the family before the divorce suit? I show you Exhibit A, which purports to be an affidavit by your wife as to her fixed monthly living expenses with the children. Look at that affidavit and tell me of any items contained there which you feel are inaccurate.

Custody

If the discovery issue relates to custody of the children, the following are some questions that might be asked:

Who prepares the meals for the children?

Are they served breakfast every morning?

What is a typical day for you as the mother of the children, starting with your getting up in the morning?

Doesn't the father frequently prepare meals for the children?

What is the quality of his cooking as compared to yours?

Doesn't he frequently bathe the children and put them to bed because you are out of the home?

Did you have any conversation with your next-door neighbor within the preceding sixty days regarding your intentions to leave the state with the children?

With whom did you travel when you took the children to Florida for spring vacation earlier this year?

Have the children given you any indication as to the parent with whom they prefer to live following the divorce?

Do any of the children have any physical or emotional disabilities or special problems?

Who is principally involved in the discipline of the children?

Calling your attention to on or about June of 1979, did you strike your daughter with a leather belt?

Who was present when this occurred?

Who has knowledge of the allegations that you have made regarding your husband's improper treatment of the children?

Is it not true that your husband is the person in your household who is principally involved with the everyday care of the children?

Is it not true that during the past year you have been away from the home on an average of three to five evenings per week?

What if anything has your wife ever done which you feel is detrimental to the children's best interests?

Who would you have care for the children while you are at work if you were to be awarded their custody?

Are there services which your wife provides for the children which you cannot?

Why haven't you provided these services in the past?

to the question. The objection may also be to the *form* of the question, if it is confusing or improper for some other reason. Your lawyer may instruct you to answer the question over his objection, preserving that objection for the trial, where the judge can then rule whether or not you should have had to answer it. If he rules that you should not, that answer cannot be used in the trial to discredit you.

If your lawyer instructs you not to answer a question at the deposition, don't answer it. The questioner may continue with other questions, or he may recess the deposition and file a petition to require that you answer the questions objected to. If the court rules that your refusal was arbitrary or unfounded, fees and court costs may be assessed against you.

CAUTION: If you are apprehensive about certain questions that may be asked at the deposition, discuss them with your lawyer beforehand. He can help you give truthful answers that do the least damage to your case.

133. Should I volunteer documents and information which are not specifically requested at the discovery deposition?

In almost every case, no. Do not show the other side *all* the evidence you have at the deposition. Don't be concerned if your own lawyer does not ask you the questions that you want him to ask, or doesn't ask for the documents that you feel will prove your case. That information will be held in reserve for use at an appropriate time. If your case must go to trial, *surprise* is one of the best weapons in your lawyer's trial arsenal. That is not to say that you should create surprise by withholding information or making false statements, but you can "breast your cards" until a specific request is made to see them.

134. Are there benefits from depositions other than the discovery of information and the preservation of testimony?

Definitely. A deposition helps you and your lawyer prepare for a possible trial in a variety of ways:
1. It helps you evaluate your spouse as a witness.
2. It may give you your first experience as a witness.
3. You will get a feeling for the strengths and weaknesses of both your spouse's case and your own.
4. The vulnerability and nervousness people commonly feel at the deposition can make them more amenable to settlement in preference to trial.
5. After the taking of depositions your lawyer should be able to give you an *informed* evaluation of your case.
6. The deposition is a natural setting for settlement discussions.

Even when you feel you don't really need more discovery information, a deposition will sometimes start things rolling by bringing the lawyers and the parties together in a four-way conference setting. Since one of the primary rules of negotiating is not to negotiate until you have all the relevant facts at your disposal, the moment the depositions are completed may be the first opportunity for you all to realistically discuss settlement.

135. Will my lawyer tell me how well I handled the deposition?

If he doesn't tell you, ask him. He may have noticed something that will help or hurt in a trial setting—but forgotten to mention it. An honest critique can be reassuring and educational.

136. Are psychological evaluations part of the discovery procedure?

Yes, if someone's mental or emotional well-being is at issue. Most state courts have provisions for voluntary or involuntary psychiatric examinations in connection with matrimonial matters. Local law decides who pays for the examination. An independent psychiatric evaluation is extremely important if there is a serious question of mental health in connection with a custody or visitation issue.

137. How should I prepare for a psychiatric evaluation?

There's probably nothing you can really do in preparation, other than to be as calm as possible and honest in your responses to questions. Don't try to "psych out" the evaluator. He does this kind of thing every day and routinely will pick up your attempts to fool him or influence his opinion during an interview. Standard psychiatric tests have built-in safeguards against manipulation by the person being tested. If you attempt to manipulate an evaluation, the test results will probably not be favorable.

138. Is it possible to obtain a second psychiatric opinion?

Yes, when a psychiatric evaluation favors one party on a particular issue, such as child custody, counsel for the other parent can obtain a second psychiatric opinion, which may differ substantially. Having experienced this conflict of psychiatric experts time and again, some trial judges give little weight to *any* psychiatric evaluation unless a serious psychiatric condition is involved.

The results of standard psychological tests are sometimes given more weight in the diagnosis of a specific psychiatric condition because they are less subjective. The more confused a judge becomes from conflicting psychiatric opinions, the more likely he will ignore them and fall back on his own experience and common sense in making the final judgment.

139. What is a social-service report?

Many divorce courts have the use of a social-service agency to make home investigations in child-custody disputes. Typically, the investigator interviews the parties, neighbors, teachers, and administrative personnel at the children's school, and also the children themselves, to decide which parent offers the better environment. A written report is then sent either to the court or the lawyers. While these reports are designed to assist in making the custodial decisions, in many jurisdictions the judge is not allowed to read them. The investigator must testify in court and be subject to cross-examination to determine the accuracy and validity of the information or opinions presented. Normally, these investigative reports should not contain opinions as to who should get custody, but they frequently do.

140. How do I prepare for social-service investigations?

The investigator will probably visit your home. Your personal appearance, standards of housekeeping, and the appearance of your children in terms of cleanliness and quality of clothing will be noted. If you are given advance notice of the visit, it doesn't hurt to put your best foot forward by showing the home environment at its *realistic best*, but don't go overboard. Don't create a phony environment where the children wear their Sunday best on a Thursday afternoon, and your home is so neat it looks as if no one lives there. Try to have your children present at the interview if you relate well to them. Keep them away if you don't or if you can't control them.

141. Shouldn't every case be uncontested?

Not necessarily. A fair settlement requires reasonable compromise. If one side is being arbitrary or makes unreasonable demands, a fair settlement may not be possible unless the other spouse shows a willingness to contest the matter and have a judge make the decision. It should be clear that you are willing to go to court if you have to. Otherwise, if it appears that you *won't* go to court, no matter what the circumstances, you severely handicap your lawyer in the negotiation and may even *encourage* excessive demands by the other spouse. If the other side remains unreasonable, then you can proceed to trial as the final alternative.

THINKING SETTLEMENT: NEGOTIATION STRATEGIES AND TECHNIQUES

142. What is unique about the negotiating in a divorce settlement?

People involved in a divorce usually are so emotional it alters normal priorities, clouds judgment, and causes them to take positions which frequently do not even represent their own best interests.

For most clients their divorce is their first contact with a lawyer or the court system. The uncertainty of the future, the possibility of permanent estrangement from children, new financial obligations and living arrangements—all arouse fear and a sense of insecurity and loss.

For example, guilt is a major emotional factor in most divorces where one party is anxious to have the marriage dissolved and the other is not. The "guilty" party usually is willing to give more and to ask for less in an effort to expiate those feelings. When the guilt feelings subside, the unfair settlement is regretted and the lawyer is usually blamed. "Why did he let me do that?" the client complains. "I was sold out." By the same token, guilt is exploited by the "wronged" spouse, who feels angry, frustrated, or self-righteous. Virtually no settlement is good enough for the angry client who wants revenge. Such an attitude can lead to expensive and protracted legal procedures with little gained.

Another unique quality of matrimonial negotiations is that there are no objective standards of success. The best result is not necessarily getting the most or paying the least. Spouses who haven't been dealt with fairly have a tendency to try to even up either through not complying or by trying to modify the decree. Since the parties often continue to have some sort of relationship because of children or some continuing obligation under the decree, a burdensome or inequitable settlement will only sustain acrimony.

143. What are matrimonial settlements based on?

They are based on the respective settlement priorities of the parties balanced by legal norms or standards of fairness in your community. Once your lawyer knows all the facts, he formulates an anticipated result as if the case were tried in court—the legal norm. He then negotiates to achieve your priorities without settling for *less* than the legal norm. If *both* parties feel a little disappointed at the result, the settlement is probably a fair one.

Some mediators say that settlements should be based entirely on the priorities or wishes of the spouses without regard to legal standards of fairness. The problem is that without knowledge of what one is entitled to, a party cannot intelligently agree to accept less than the legal norm. *Informed* consent is essential where emotions may control the bargaining.

144. What are the ingredients of a successful negotiation?

Any successful negotiation requires:
1. Proper timing.
2. Adequate preparation.
3. A credible negotiating position.

Proper timing requires that the parties be psychologically ready for the divorce. Otherwise they will resist any serious negotiation. The clients also should be ready to negotiate *realistically*, rather than emotionally or arbitrarily. If you negotiate at the wrong time, you will not only accomplish nothing, but you will lose the advantage by showing your cards too soon. Since *you* are more likely to be emotional or arbitrary than your lawyer, let *him* do the negotiating for you and determine the proper timing for that negotiation.

Adequate preparation requires knowledge of all the relevant facts, the leverage factors, and your priorities.

A *credible negotiating position* means that your demands and the reasons for them are not arbitrary, unrealistic, or untruthful. Only when both sides are credible can you have *serious* negotiations, not merely posturing and jockeying for a dominant position.

145. What are legally relevant facts of a case?

The facts that must be proved for you to gain the legal result you seek. The laws of your state regarding the division of property, for example, will determine what facts, such as title or financial contribution, are relevant in the division of a marital home or of stocks and bonds. Because laws vary from state to state, what may be relevant to establish your legal right to the home in New York may be quite different in California.

Being unfamiliar with the law, you are more inclined to think of relevance in terms of emotional or psychological issues rather than legal proof requirements. If you are seeking an award of the marital residence, legally relevant facts relate to: 1) title; 2) source of financial contribution; and 3) personal improvement to the property. Legally *irrelevant* facts relate to: 1) character of the parties; 2) marital misconduct; and 3) innocence of a party.

146. What is psychological relevance?

This broader relevance takes into account emotional needs and the personal *priorities* of the clients. These may have nothing to do with the law, but a great deal to do with the final settlement agreement. All settlements involve the use of leverage factors. A knowledge of the other spouse's priorities and emotional needs may constitute important psychological leverage factors.

For instance, a fear of litigation, a wish to remarry, an obsession for owning a particular item of marital property are all factors which are psychologically relevant, because they can be used to pressure or to gain leverage in negotiation concessions.

147. How do legal and psychological leverage factors affect the settlement?

Anything you control that the other side wants, or vice versa, becomes a leverage factor.

In a fault state the most important legal leverage factor is often the question of who wants the divorce more. If grounds cannot be proved, the other party may be able to delay or defeat a divorce unless the person seeking it makes substantial concessions in order to get it. If your spouse wants it (remarriage, a quick divorce; a move to another state), and you can deny it or delay it—that is a psychological leverage factor. If the facts of your case point to a particular legal result—that is a legal leverage factor.

The art of negotiation is the ability to perceive and use these leverage factors to obtain concessions. Since both sides usually have something the other side wants, these factors are traded like chips. The side with more leverage can obtain more concessions in the trading process. The end result of the trades and compromises is the settlement.

148. Do plans to remarry affect the settlement negotiations?

Yes, but the manner and extent of the effect depend on the unresolved issues in your case. If, for example, your spouse knows you are eager to remarry, *delay* becomes a leverage factor pressuring you to accept a lesser settlement. Your spouse may purposely delay the resolution of your case for that reason.

In most states, you will not be entitled to alimony after remarriage unless your settlement agreement provides to the contrary. If you are awarded property in lieu of alimony without advising the other side of your immediate intention to remarry, the property award can be set aside in some states on grounds of fraud. The theory is that the court never would have awarded you property in lieu of maintenance (or your spouse never would have agreed to give it to you) if they had been aware of your intention to remarry.

149. When are we prepared to negotiate?

When five requirements have been met:
1. Your lawyer must have the *authority* from you to negotiate.
2. Your lawyer should have all the facts, financial and otherwise, that bear upon the negotiations. The discovery process should be essentially completed. He should also know the law as it applies to those facts.
3. Your lawyer should know all the items or issues to be negotiated in your case. The settlement should be complete, with no unresolved items.
4. Your lawyer should know your priorities regarding those bargaining items. What is it you *really* want, not what you may *say* you want. He or she should know your spouse's priorities, too, in order to recognize a bluff and to put pressure in the area of greatest vulnerability. Certain items may be so cherished that you or your spouse value them far and above their intrinsic value. Those are priority items that form the bottom line below which you will not go.

(This knowledge represents what was referred to as the psychologically relevant factors.)

5. Your lawyer must be aware of the significant *leverage factors* that bear upon the negotiations—your leverage factors as well as your spouse's.

Once these five requirements are met, you and your lawyer are prepared to negotiate. Since timing is the key to successful negotiation, a failure to meet any of these requirements will result in premature negotiations—a less successful settlement or no settlement at all.

150. How do we determine what subjects should be included in the settlement agreement?

We have already discussed many of the possible areas to be included in a settlement. If you have children, custody and visitation must be decided. If you have property, it must be distributed. If you have inherited a summer house and are sentimentally attached to it, this is a bargaining subject. Furniture, summer camp, cars, all can be bargaining subjects—areas in dispute. They may not all be apparent at first, but will emerge as negotiations begin and information is accumulated.

A settlement agreement should be complete—no loose ends or unresolved problems. Every issue to be resolved, every item of property to be exchanged should be considered and provided for. Where do you start? Where it hurts the most. Treat the deepest wound first, then move on to the scratches.

It is easy to overlook items, though, and for that reason, we have compiled a comprehensive Settlement Considerations Check List on the following page. Check off any that may apply to your case.

There is always a temptation to defer, until *after* the divorce, certain touchy issues which you don't want to raise now. Who pays for parochial school, or your move to another state, or the fact that you are three months pregnant and haven't told anyone? Discuss the issue with your lawyer. Some hidden issues, if raised now, could be used as powerful leverage against you. But most of these touchy issues will be more difficult to resolve later, when you don't have as many unresolved issues to trade. The test is when will your *leverage* be better? Don't forget the cost, either. Litigation after a decree can cost more than your divorce.

151. Is it more important that my lawyer be a good settlor or a good trial lawyer?

The most successful matrimonial lawyers are the best settlors. A negotiated settlement is far more likely to result in a satisfactory

84

fee for the lawyer and a reasonably satisfied client. Protracted litigation has diminishing returns for both you and your lawyer.

The lawyer's ultimate skill is the art of resolving the apparently unresolvable through negotiation and compromise. His or her trial skills will affect the negotiation if the other side is aware that he *can* and *will* try the case in court if negotiation demands are arbitrary or unrealistic. In other words, the lawyer must have the skill to negotiate the fair result without a trial—but he must be willing and able to try the case in order to achieve that fair result. The trial is his six-gun, which he hopes he won't have to use to keep the peace.

Although a trial specialist can be brought in at the last moment if negotiations fail, the best lawyers are skilled at both negotiation and trial. (You should find out at the initial interview whether your lawyer is able and willing to go to trial if necessary.)

152. Are the tough negotiations the most successful ones in divorce cases?

No single method is the most successful, and the best negotiators can be hard or soft, as a particular case demands. Whether or not the lawyer is a hard or soft negotiator, a puncher or a counter-puncher, a leader or a follower in terms of negotiating techniques, he must still properly employ the factors of timing, preparation, and credibility to be successful.

SETTLEMENT CONSIDERATIONS CHECK LIST
(Divorce Decree Outline)

Consult Glossary for technical terms.

I. *Introduction:*
Recitals identifying the parties, the attorneys, and whether the resolution was agreed or the result of a contest trial.

II. *Findings:*
The extent of required factual determinations (findings) will vary from state to state and may involve the technique of the draftsman.
A. Residence or domicile of the parties (place and duration).
B. Date and place of marriage.
C. Names and birth dates of children (born or adopted).
D. Fitness of one or both parents for child custody or visitation.
E. Reason for the divorce (irretrievable breakdown of the marriage, marital misconduct, or other grounds accepted in your state).

III. *Order or Judgment of the court on the issues:*
If there is a written or oral agreement, it is recited or physically attached as the judgment of the court, once the judge has approved or accepted it.

A. BONDS OF MATRIMONY ARE DISSOLVED

B. CHILDREN:
1. Custody (single-parent, joint, split).
2. Visitation (general or specific, notice of change).
3. Support Items:
    a. Weekly, monthly, or semimonthly *support* payment; duration, modifiability, suspension during extended visitation.
    b. Ordinary and extraordinary *medical*/dental-expense liability; prior notice; health insurance.
    c. Liability for *education* costs; private school, college, trade or graduate school; authority to select school; access to school records.
    d. Maintenance of *life insurance* for children's benefit; amount, duration, trustee or custodian for proceeds; right to borrow on or switch policies; possession of policies and proof of maintenance.
    e. Testamentary provisions for children (*wills*).

     f. Liability for lessons, summer camp, religious train-
ing, special needs of disabled children, or other
special costs.

     g. Dependency *exemption*—who claims for this year's
and future years' income tax?

4. Agreement or restrictions against *removal* of children's
residence to another jurisdiction or state.

5. *Restraints* on third-party contact (paramours, friends
who may be bad influence) or detrimental activities
for children (stay out of taverns, no parachuting).

6. *Rights* of relatives such as grandparents or other interested third parties to contact with the children.

7. *Sharing* of vital information and/or decisions regarding health and education.

8. *Telephone contact*—rights or restrictions in connection
with frequency and cost of calls by children or parents.

C. SPOUSAL SUPPORT (alimony/maintenance)

1. Lump-sum or periodic-installment payments for fixed
or indefinite period.

2. *Amount,* duration, allocation.

3. *Modifiability* as to amount or duration in the event of:
disability, death, or retirement of husband or wife; remarriage of wife; cohabitation of wife; employment of
wife; material change in financial condition of husband or wife; emancipation of children.

4. *Security* for unpaid installments in the event of payor's
death or disability (life insurance, securities, other).

5. *Tax effect* of payments.

6. *Escalator* or de-escalator clauses (automatic increase
or decrease).

7. Option to *accelerate* payments.

8. Option to *convert* periodic payments to a lesser lump
sum at a later date in the event of remarriage of recipient.

9. *Life insurance* (amount, duration, policy ownership,
beneficiary).

10. Liability for *medical and dental* (ordinary and extraordinary); maintenance or conversion of health insurance to individual coverage.

11. Right to *work* (effect on alimony or child support).

12. Testamentary provisions (*wills,* inheritances).

D. PROPERTY DIVISION

1. Whether division is in addition to or in lieu of alimony.

Settlement Considerations Check List, continued.

2. Disposition of *real estate*:
   a. Residence—Sale, title change, or exclusive possession in one spouse (how long, or subject to what conditions); division of proceeds on sale—what credits to be given for mortgage reduction or improvements).
   b. Other real estate—vacation home, rental property, business property, tax-shelter real estate partnerships.
   c. Leaseholds—who is liable for payments, entitled to security deposit, entitled to possession?
   d. Maintenance, repair, insurance costs, real estate taxes, etc.; who is responsible?
   e. Tax liability for capital gains in connection with transfer of appreciated property; deferrability of gain in connection with principal residence.
   f. Liability for existing and future mortgages, liens, and encumbrances.
   g. Method of conveying real estate (warranty or quit-claim deed).
3. Disposition of *bank accounts* and high-interest investments:
   a. Checking and savings accounts.
   b. Money-market accounts, certificates of deposit, treasury bills or notes, commercial paper.
   c. Who declares interest for income-tax purposes?
4. Disposition of *securities* and corporate holdings:
   a. Is there joint, marital, or community ownership?
   b. Are transfers to be made in kind, in exchange for other assets, or as a division of sale proceeds?
   c. Value of transferred and retained shares.
   d. Tax liability for long- and short-term gains.
5. Disposition of *partnerships*, joint ventures, sole proprietorships and other business entities:
   a. Is there joint marital or community ownership?
   b. Value of interest transferred, retained, or released.
   c. Tax liability for long- or short-term gains.
6. Disposition of miscellaneous personal property:
   a. Pensions, profit sharing, annuities, and IRA accounts (present value; current setoff, or deferred payment).
   b. Household furnishings, tools, gardening equipment, personal effects (description of items; time and manner of delivery).

c. Antiques, art, collections, and jewelry.

d. Club memberships (use and division of equity).

e. Disposition of property in revocable trusts or held by third parties as security; accounts receivable.

f. Disposition of vehicles and boats—payment of loans on these.

g. Disposition of royalties, copyrights, patents, or causes of action (lawsuits not brought to judgment).

E. DEBTS

1. *Schedule of creditors* and balances due.
2. *Who will assume?* As of when?
3. Liability for *debts omitted* from schedule.
4. Disposition of *security* where one spouse is to pay off secured debt.
5. Liability for current and past *income taxes,* assessments, and penalties.
6. *Indemnification* and hold harmless in connection with debts to be paid by other spouse.

F. MISCELLANEOUS OPTIONAL PROVISIONS

1. Resumption of *maiden* or former name.
2. Whether written agreement is to be *incorporated and merged* in the final decree or remain separate (affects modifiability and certain tax effects of alimony).
3. *Restraining orders* prohibiting certain conduct (such as altering insurance beneficiaries, etc.).
4. *Arbitration* clause—agreement to arbitrate future disputes out of court.
5. *Tax returns*—whether or not to be filed jointly for tax year preceding divorce, as well as indemnification from liability.
6. *Security* clause—penalty, setoff, abatement, or funding devices to secure mutual compliance with certain provisions of the decree.
7. Attorney fees and costs—amount, who pays, and when.
8. Attorney fees in event of noncompliance—who pays, and under what circumstances.
9. Release and waiver of claims against the other spouse's property, income and estate, past, present, or future, except as set forth in the decree.
10. *Execution* of documents—time and manner to effectuate provisions of decree.

SETTLEMENT PRIORITIES WORKSHEET

Make a list like this one before you enter into negotiations:

A. My priorities in terms of the children are:

1.
2.
3.

B. My spouse's priorities are:

1.
2.
3.

C. My priorities in terms of support are:

1.
2.
3.

D. My spouse's priorities are:

1.
2.
3.

E. My priorities in terms of property division are:

1.
2.
3.
4.
5:

F. My spouse's priorities are:

1.
2.
3.
4.
5:

TALKING SETTLEMENT: SETTLEMENT CONFERENCES AND PRETRIAL HEARINGS

153. What is mediation?

Mediation is a voluntary procedure where a couple submits their dispute to a specially trained individual (or team) who helps them reach a settlement. Most mediators are lawyers or mental health professionals, but their role is to *guide* rather than to give advice or treat therapy. People should not enter mediation unless they have determined to dissolve their marriage. A mediated agreement is not binding until it has been presented to the court and approved for entry as a judgment.

154. Do we need lawyers if we mediate?

Yes. Even if the mediator is a lawyer, he or she is not permitted to give legal advice. Although it is not legally required, it is recommended that each spouse have independent legal counsel from the outset of the mediation. In most cases, the lawyers will not be present at the mediation sessions but will help in the discovery process and give legal advice as needed. Mediators who discourage the retention of counsel until the mediation is completed cannot avoid giving legal advice. One person advising two parties with conflicting interests is ethically improper and in-creases the chance that the mediated agreement will fall apart once the lawyers review it.

155. Is mediation faster or less expensive than the normal manner of resolving divorce disputes?

Probably not. Mediators often claim their system is quicker and cheaper, but they are comparing a successful mediation with a contested divorce. If the issues to be mediated are complex, the parties must pay for both the attorneys and the mediator. If the issues are simple, a lawyer can help the parties reach an agree-ment and complete the court proceedings without the expense of a mediator. If the mediation is unsuccessful, you will still have to pay the mediator's fee and start over again with attorneys. Since there is no way to predict the outcome of mediation, it is hard to general-ize about its speed or cost.

156. What are the advantages or disadvantages of mediation?

Proponents of mediation claim that their system has one or more of the following advantages over the adversarial system:

1. The process is less adversarial, therefore less stressful to the spouses and their children.

2. The therapeutic model in communication, cooperation, and compromise enhances the ongoing relationship of the parties and their ability to resolve future problems. Even where the mediation is unsuccessful, there is a therapeutic "halo effect" that results in a greater willingness to cooperate and compromise.

3. The use of mental health professionals as mediators adds greater sensitivity to client needs and a superior ability to deal with emotional conflicts in the negotiation process.

4. Mediation is better suited for the resolution of child-custody and visitation disputes, where the best interests of the child, rather than those of the parents, should be the goal.

5. Mediated settlements are more creative because the input of the spouses is not inhibited by traditional legal approaches.

6. The spouses derive greater satisfaction from the results of mediation than from trials or adversarial settlements because they can give more input and have better control of the process.

7. Mediated settlements result in greater compliance and less relitigation because of the personal investment of the spouses.

8. Successful mediations are quicker because the emphasis on cooperation and compromise encourages early resolution of dis-puted issues. Less time is spent on discovery and negotiation-posturing than is common to the adversarial system.

9. Successful mediations are cheaper because less time and formal discovery are involved, and one mediator costs less than two attorneys.

10. Mediation provides an alternative for consumers which may have a competitive market effect on price.

Those who oppose mediation or support it with reservations suggest some of the following problems:

1. A nonattorney cannot mediate property and support disputes without a thorough knowledge of local law and settlement norms.

2. Ethical problems arise where an attorney-mediator gives legal advice to both parties when they have conflicting interests. A co-mediation with a nonattorney may also raise an ethical problem if the attorney is considered to be practicing law with the layman. The layman-mediator will be guilty of unauthorized practice of law if legal advice is given in the course of mediation. Since it is impossible to mediate any but the simplest marital dispute without knowledge of local legal norms, a lawyer must be available to assist the layman-mediator, and two lawyers may be required to avoid conflict-of-interest problems. In the truly simple cases, a mediator is an unnecessary expense.

3. Mediators tend to emphasize *settlement* over *fair settlement* in an effort to achieve a successful mediation.

4. A mediator whose success is based on achieving settlement is more likely to give in to overreaching, or to overlook unfairness when one spouse is arbitrary. Adversarial procedures provide a check and balance in this situation.

5. Mediation requires and presumes good faith and honesty on the part of the participants. In fact, the more serious the marital dispute, the more justified the spouses feel in lying, cheating, and stealing to protect what is "rightfully theirs." If the mediator relies on trust rather than on a healthy skepticism, the dishonest or manipulating spouse will have a distinct advantage.

6. Unless attorneys are employed from the outset, mediation discovery is generally inadequate, and the parties' consent is often uninformed.

7. Two lawyers experienced in family law can be expected to come up with more settlement alternatives and more creative use of the tax laws than a single mediator.

8. A mediator who does not represent either party cannot provide the emotional support and security available from an attorney who protects his client's interest in the dispute.

9. Unsuccessful mediations are more expensive and require an unscrambling of the egg as the parties proceed to litigate after undergoing the expense of the mediation.

10. If the case is simple, one attorney can draft a settlement

and prove it up in court faster than a mediator, who must refer the couple to an attorney once the mediation is completed.

157. Can all cases be mediated?

No. The likelihood of a successful mediation depends principally upon the honesty of the participants, their willingness to compromise personal priorities to reach a fair settlement, and the skill of the mediator. The emotionalism and antagonism common to divorcing couples as well as their lack of equal knowledge and bargaining strength reduce the number of cases which are truly appropriate for mediation. A skilled mediator will generally spot the couples who are not good candidates for mediation, and so advise them at the initial meeting. Mediation does appear to be particularly appropriate to resolve custody and visitation disputes, and many court-sponsored programs are springing up around the country to mediate rather than litigate child-oriented issues.

158. What is a settlement conference?

It is any meeting between lawyers or lawyers and clients for the purpose of resolving disputed issues. The time and place for these conferences are generally planned in advance, after discovery is complete, but they often occur spontaneously as an outgrowth of a deposition or court hearing. The spontaneous conference is often the most successful because it is motivated by a mutual desire to "get this over with." That attitude is a key settlement ingredient because it suggests a willingness to compromise.

159. What is a pretrial hearing?

It is an informal conference with a judge as mediator. There are two kinds of pretrials: One is purely a settlement conference to resolve anything from a single issue to the entire case; the other is a meeting between the lawyers and the judge immediately prior to trial for the purpose of narrowing disputed issues to be tried. This chapter deals with the settlement before the trial. Chapter XIII deals with the conference to narrow issues.

160. What is the purpose of the judge's presence, if he cannot order the settlement?

Influence: The judge has influence over the lawyers and the clients because of his official position. The pretrial is an opportunity to learn how a judge would rule on a given factual situation without placing yourself in the jeopardy of a final trial ruling. It is

94

a way to test the water without jumping in. Even when the judge's suggestion is the same as your lawyer's prediction, you are likely to be more influenced by the black robe.

Lack of bias: The pretrial judge can also be helpful in forcing a party or a lawyer who has been arbitrary in the settlement negotiations to be more reasonable.

For example, a wife may believe that she is entitled to one half of her husband's income for alimony because that is what her friend received or what her mother said she deserved. On the other hand, her husband may believe she should get a job because his boss is a woman. Emotionally distraught clients frequently hear only what they want to hear—the outcome most favorable to *them.* The pretrial judge can dispel any misconceptions because he regularly decides divorce disputes and can predict the outcome of your case with authority and without bias.

161. When do pretrial hearings occur?

Whenever the lawyers or the judge wants them to occur. You could be in court on a temporary support motion and the judge might ask the lawyers to step into his chambers to see if the motion could better be resolved informally with his assistance. Often, if the parties have come before him on a variety of temporary motions, the judge may suggest that the lawyers and parties sit down with him to try and resolve the entire case.

Some courts have pretrial judges who do nothing but conduct informal negotiation sessions in an attempt to resolve the entire case. This kind of settlement conference is generally arranged by the lawyers by mutual agreement after their discovery is complete and after their own settlement negotiations have either failed or achieved only partial success.

162. What information is needed for the pretrial hearing?

Facts: Your lawyer should have a sufficient grasp of the facts, both financial and personal, so that he can employ leverage factors to your best advantage. In most cases, negotiations have occurred before the pretrial, so only the areas of dispute need be presented to the pretrial judge.

Memorandum: Some judges require some form of written memorandum outlining pertinent personal and financial data, as well as the issues to be resolved at the pretrial. Whether required or not, a simple written summary of finances and disputed issues is always an effective way to help the judge understand *your* side of the case. While the other lawyer is arguing the merits of his case, you will often find the judge glancing at the written memorandum.

95

Written memoranda should be exchanged between the two sides before the pretrial to verify accuracy.

163. How is the pretrial hearing conducted?

In most cases the hearing occurs in the judge's chambers. The lawyers go in first, without their clients, to give the judge a summary of the case up to that point. Usually the judge is concerned with only the financial factors that are in dispute, rather than with the grounds. However, if you are in a fault state, or if misconduct has bearing on the division of property, child custody, or support, the lawyer should make the misconduct leverage factors known to the judge.

The lawyers give the judge any memoranda they have prepared, and then each one summarizes his client's position orally. The judge may question the lawyers for more details or may challenge the legal bases for a particular settlement demand. The judge may "lean on" one or both lawyers by disputing the reasonableness of some position they are taking. If the lawyer gives in to the judge's pressure, a balancing compromise may be sought from the other lawyer, and certain alternatives suggested. Whether the lawyers and judge are strangers or have worked together hundreds of times, a great deal of strategy and technique is involved in getting to what the lawyers maintain is their client's bottom line—the minimum settlement they will accept.

The next step is for the judge to interview the parties together or individually with their lawyers. (Most judges prefer to interview each of the parties with their lawyer present.) During the interview, the judge gauges the personalities of the parties: some respond best to a soft, reasoning approach; other to a hard, authoritative technique. Some need to be smiled at; others, threatened. Security is the key word with some litigants; jeopardy or fear with others. In any event, the judge, by his own statements and reaction to others', begins the process of persuading the parties or attorneys to compromise their stated demands.

To be effective, the judge may orchestrate the meeting so that, for example, he suggests to the husband, privately, that a trial judge might award as much as $1,000 per month alimony; and then, in his conference with the wife, suggests that the trial might only bring $700 per month. His intention, of course, is that the parties agree to something in between. The judge is not being dishonest, in that there is only a *range* for support, and precise predictions are impossible. A reminder of the extremes can be intimidating to the parties, so compromise becomes a more attractive alternative.

It is essential that the pretrial judge be both knowledgeable as to the law and impartial as to the parties. If he lacks either quality, his effectiveness will be undermined. The clients will not be impressed nor persuaded to compromise. The lawyers will discourage their clients' acceptance of judicial suggestions that appear out of line with their experience.

164. Why aren't all the pretrial negotiations out in the open, with everyone present before the judge?

At various stages, private negotiations are more effective. The pretrial may involve a series of separate *and* joint consultations in and out of the chambers to confer with counsel or the judge before compromising on various points. You may prefer to confer privately with your lawyer in matters of strategy or confidence and may prefer private interviews with the judge for the same reason. You and your lawyer and the judge will speak with greater candor when your spouse is not present. The greater your feeling of confidence in the judge—that he *understands* your side of the case—the more susceptible you will be to his persuasion.

JUDGE: "I'm beginning to appreciate what you've gone through, Mrs. Smith. Your husband is a *very* difficult man to deal with. It might be worth it to take a little less of the property than you're entitled to, just to avoid further aggravation."

MRS. SMITH: "I'm so glad you understand, Your Honor. Everyone thinks he's so considerate. But they don't have to live with him every day. How much do you think you could get him to give me?"

JUDGE: "Well, it's hard to say. His offer is ridiculous, and I wouldn't let you accept it. On the other hand, we don't want to drag you through these courts for months just to prove you're right. How about if I can get him to pay $20,000 and not a penny less. Would you be willing to take it?"

MRS. SMITH: "Oh, thank you, Your Honor. It's less than I expected, but if you think it's fair . . ."

The lawyer then either: 1) suggests they step outside because he thinks the judge is way out of line and wants the client to hold out; or 2) he covers his previously too-high prediction by reluctantly agreeing "out of respect for the judge and in the interests of harmony," etc; or 3) he agrees enthusiastically because the judge's recommendation mirrors his own and the client needs encouragement.

165. Can there be more than one pretrial hearing?

Yes. Often a series of pretrial hearings is necessary because it takes time to soften the position of people who are adamant. The passage of time can be a great settlor. Tempers cool, circumstances and attitudes change, new relationships develop, and new perspectives are gained. Even though you may feel the initial pretrial hearing was a waste of time because no one substantially altered his or her position, the seeds of a change in attitude may have been planted. This will make compromise easier later on.

The lawyers should use the time between pretrial hearings to reconsider and perhaps restructure their clients' demands to give them a fresh look when they are next before a pretrial judge. Restructuring the agreement for a client whose pride keeps him or her from compromising will allow change without loss of face.

Again, knowledge of the priorities of both parties is essential to structuring subtle changes in negotiation positions. For example, if a desire to remain in the same house until the children finish school is of greater priority to a parent than money from the sale of the home, a demand for full ownership might be restructured to a half or three-quarter share of sale proceeds deferred for the required number of years.

166. What if my lawyer tells me the settlement is unfair, but I want to settle anyway?

Ultimately, you make the decision, but a knowledgeable lawyer will properly discourage you from accepting an unfair agreement. Many clients persist anyway from feelings of guilt, anxiety over pending litigation, or a desire to remarry. In many cases, clients who enter into a substantially unfair settlement may in the future blame the lawyer. If you insist on such an agreement, your lawyer may require you to put in writing that you accept the settlement contrary to his advice. This protects the lawyer from a later claim that the client was sold out or somehow misadvised.

CAUTION: If you have a serious dispute with your lawyer about the fairness of a settlement proposal, or suspect that he prefers trials to settlements, seek a second opinion from another lawyer, not a friend or relative.

167. How do I know whether to accept a proposed settlement or keep on negotiating?

While you may know what you want, you're never sure what you can get. That's why your lawyer's advice is crucial at this point. Regardless of which lawyer drafted the settlement proposal, break down its details into separate items and number them consecutively: 1) custody; 2) visitation; 3) support; etc.

Next, consider the questions in the following check list. Ask your lawyer those questions that relate to a particular item on your list or to the agreement as a whole.

QUESTIONS TO ASK YOUR LAWYER WHEN CONSIDERING A SPECIFIC SETTLEMENT PROPOSITION

When discovery has been completed to the point where you are ready to negotiate seriously, write down the details of any settlement proposal and number the items consecutively. Then, regardless of who is making the offer, consider the following questions for your attorney.

1. In what way is this settlement better or worse than what a court is likely to order if we go to trial?
2. What are the advantages or disadvantages of settling now, as opposed to waiting for trial?
3. Which elements of the settlement do you feel are most important to the other side?
4. Which elements of their offer do you feel are negotiable?
5. Are there any particular elements of their offer that you feel are arbitrary or unfair?
6. Is the amount of money from property division and alimony going to be reduced or otherwise affected by income taxes? If so, how much?
7. Is this the complete settlement or are there other items that will be added later?
8. In order to resolve the simple issues, are there items in this settlement offer that we can agree to leaving aside with the unresolved items to be determined by the court?
9. How long will it take to finish the case if we don't settle now? If we do settle now?
10. Do you recommend that we make a counter-offer or delay in some way, if the delay works to our advantage?
11. Is there anything I can do (or stop doing) that will improve our settlement possibilities?
12. Do you feel the settlement is fair, or *better* than fair?
13. Will you be upset, as my attorney, if I refuse this offer? Why?
14. If you were in my place would you accept this offer? If not, why?

168. Can every case be settled before trial?

No. Some cases can *never* be settled, due either to the personalities of the individuals involved or to an honest disagreement as to facts or interpretation of the law. This disagreement then can only be resolved by trial. Where only certain issues are disputed, it is possible to try those issues and agree on the rest.

Chapter **XIII**

PREPARING
FOR TRIAL

169. Do trials take place in states that have no-fault divorce laws?

Yes. While the grounds for divorce may not have to be contested, all other issues that cannot be resolved must be presented to the court for trial. Questions of child custody, visitation, property division, support, and alimony all require trial preparation and presentation in accordance with the procedures and rules of evidence in effect in your jurisdiction.

170. What if my lawyer suggests that another lawyer be hired for the trial?

Such a suggestion means your lawyer is either tired of your case or feels inadequate to try it. In either event, look for a trial lawyer immediately. Your present lawyer will probably recommend someone. Get several names, if possible, and follow the search procedure recommended in Chapter IV.

171. Do I pay two lawyers?

Yes, unless you discharge the first one; but each lawyer is paid only for the time he or she is actively representing you.

172. What does a trial consist of?

A typical trial can be broken down into eight segments:
1. Pretrial conference: The lawyers and trial judge meet to determine what issues must be tried and what facts can be agreed on. Any issues dealing with the conduct of the trial can be discussed at this conference.
2. Opening statements: The lawyers summarize what they intend to prove to the judge. When the issues are limited, these statements are often waived.
3. Plaintiff's case: The party who originally filed suit presents evidence in support of the complaint.
4. Defendant's case: The responding party presents evidence to deny or counter the plaintiff's case.
5. Rebuttal by plaintiff: Evidence is offered to deny or counter new matter raised in the defendant's case. (This step is often unnecessary.)
6. Surrebuttal by defendant: Evidence is offered to deny or counter new matter raised in the rebuttal. (This step is unnecessary in most cases.)
7. Closing arguments: The lawyers summarize the evidence presented, in the light most favorable to their clients. Their arguments often impress clients more than they do the judge, who has probably made up his mind by this time. For that reason these arguments are often waived.
8. The judge's ruling (not necessarily on the same day the trial is over).

173. Can the conference immediately before trial be used as a settlement conference?

The trial judge *can* use the pretrial conference for a last-ditch effort at settlement. The issues cannot be examined as closely as they were at the pretrial *hearing*, because this judge's suggestions might be interpreted as prejudicial, and thereby disqualify him as the trial judge. This is often a good time to settle, because a willingness to compromise may surface for the first time. In the final preparation for trial, both lawyers and clients often realize the weaknesses in their own cases. The risk of a loss or a result less than they originally hoped for will encourage them to avoid the time and expense of a trial. The imminence of trial may also smoke out the bluffers who have held out to the last minute in the hope that the other side will make concessions.

If no settlement is reached at the pretrial conference, at least the trial judge has a better perspective of the overall case and will be better able to evaluate the evidence as it is presented.

174. Are closed hearings available in "awkward" cases?

Yes. If the parties agree to an *in camera* hearing, the judge will generally be willing to hear the matter in his chambers or some other suitable closed setting. The lawyers simply have to ask for this type of hearing, indicate why they feel it is necessary and that it is by agreement of the parties. In most cases children are interviewed or testify *in camera* outside the hearing of their parents, in order to avoid the anxiety and embarrassment of a public trial. Statutes in many states provide this protection for children without requiring the agreement of the parents.

175. Must I have witnesses?

No, but it helps. In a contested trial the burden is on you to prove your case by a preponderance of the evidence. If, however, a judge believes your testimony and feels you have proven your case by your testimony alone, no corroborating witnesses are necessary.

The *number* of witnesses presented by either side is not nearly as important as their credibility. The danger of *too many* witnesses is that one or more may be so nervous or verbally inadequate that the overall presentation of your case is diminished. Even a well-prepared witness who is outstanding in the confines of the lawyer's office can freeze on the witness stand and appear to be testifying from a poorly memorized script. One credible witness to a given event may be better than one credible and three partially credible.

Prepare a list of potential witnesses and what issues they can testify about. You and your lawyer can work from this list in selecting witnesses.

176. Should my friends or relatives testify on my behalf as character witnesses?

More than likely, your character or your spouse's is not an issue, even in fault states, where marital misconduct must be proved before a divorce will be granted. Therefore, while it is always reassuring to have such support, their testimony will only be relevant if it relates to a particular issue before the court.

102

177. Can witnesses refuse to testify?

No, not if they are subpoenaed, but if they are angry because you forced them into court, their testimony may be harmful to your case. Some witnesses ask to be subpoenaed so they will not appear to be testifying voluntarily on your behalf. They generally ask when they are on good terms with both parties. They don't want to seem to be taking sides, but feel obliged to reveal the truth. Some lawyers furnish all witnesses with subpoenas to avoid the accusation of prejudice that arises when a person testifies voluntarily.

178. Can my former lawyer or a psychiatrist who treated me refuse to testify, even if subpoenaed?

Communications between lawyers and their clients, and between psychiatrists and their patients, are privileged by statute in most states and may not be revealed unless the client or patient waives the privilege. Without this protection you might not be completely candid in your conversations with these people, and the quality of their services might suffer as a result.

You may specifically state that you waive the privilege, or you can waive it by taking some action that is inconsistent with the purpose of the privilege. For example, if someone alleges a psychological condition as proof of mental cruelty or as an excuse for certain behavior, the other side has the right to bring in the attending psychiatrist to verify that condition. If you attempt to justify certain actions by saying that your lawyer told you to do it, the privilege has been waived to the extent that the lawyer may be questioned on that particular point.

CAUTION: The law regarding privilege is a very sensitive one and varies from state to state. If a question arises in your case, your lawyer should be consulted and the statutes and case law of your jurisdiction followed. In some states, for instance, statements made to a treating psychologist or marriage counselor are privileged, even though they contain admissions directly contrary to the allegations and evidence presented to the court. Most marriage counselors will resist testifying in matrimonial matters, claiming a privilege that they may not possess. The danger in forcing them to testify is that they will usually testify favorably to the party they counseled.

179. Will my friends who will be witnesses be able to watch the trial?

At the outset of most trials one or both of the lawyers make a motion to exclude witnesses. This motion is routinely granted, and all witnesses for either side, other than the principal parties themselves, must stay out of the courtroom until it is time for them to testify. Witnesses who remain in the courtroom *after* completing their testimony cannot be recalled for rebuttal or surrebuttal testimony, and so it is good practice to ask them to leave.

The obvious purpose of excluding witnesses is to avoid changes in their testimony based on what they hear from the other testimony. Anyone who is not a witness can watch a trial unless it is conducted *in camera*.

180. Can my spouse call me as a witness?

Yes. Each party may call the other as a witness. Because it is expected that they will be hostile or uncooperative in answering questions, the opposing lawyer is given greater leeway in the form of his questions, and usually he proceeds in the same manner as if he were cross-examining.

181. Why should any witness be called who is hostile to my side of the case?

The hostile witness may be the only person possessing information which is essential to your case. Although that witness may not give you certain information, it is hoped that he will tell the truth when questioned under oath on a particular point. If he does lie, you are not responsible for his testimony, and the judge will have to weigh his credibility along with the other evidence presented on that point. A good reason for calling the opposing spouse as *your* witness may be your expectation of false statements that you have evidence to refute. If you can prove those statements false, the *overall* credibility of your spouse is undermined. Even truthful statements may be suspect after a lie has been proved.

182. How is my trial judge chosen?

The assignment procedure varies in different courts. In low-population areas, there may be only one judge who hears all cases. Larger court systems will have as many as twenty judges hearing nothing but divorce, separation, and annulment cases. Some judges will hear only temporary or postdecree motions, and some will hear trials on some system of random assignment. You may not know who your trial judge will be until the day you go to trial.

183. Can I change judges?

A Petition for Change of Venue or Substitution of Judges can be filed before trial begins if you believe that the judge to whom you are assigned is prejudiced against you, or if your lawyer knows the judge's bias will work against you. A hearing may be required before that judge to determine the validity of your charge of prejudice. In most jurisdictions you will be allowed at least one change of venue regardless of cause and without proof of prejudice.

CAUTION: Once trial has begun, a change of judge is allowed only under circumstances so extreme that a mistrial is called for.

184. Can my spouse fix the case?

Sometimes one spouse brags about being able to fix the case in order to intimidate the other. Unfortunately, most people are quite willing to believe that fixing a case is possible.

While it is naïve to suggest that *no* judges are subject to influence, in fact you rarely need consider this possibility, unless the judge's prejudice or refusal to follow the law is apparent. In that case, a change of venue or mistrial should be sought immediately.

If you are concerned about your spouse's threat to fix the case, your lawyer can write your spouse's lawyer a letter setting forth that allegation. If a case is already on trial or assigned to a trial judge, your lawyer can bring the spouse's statement to the attention of the judge, with notice to the opposing lawyer. You can expect a denial of the statement and a good deal of embarrassment. Having been put on notice of the threats, the judge is likely to bend over backward to demonstrate fairness and propriety in the handling of your case.

185. Is it proper for a lawyer to "prepare" a witness to testify?

It is negligent *not* to prepare a witness, unless the testimony is so factually limited that no possible confusion is likely.

The time and method of witness preparation vary with each lawyer. Generally, shortly before the trial, the witness comes to the lawyer's office and discusses in detail the issues of the case about which he or she has knowledge. Eyewitness accounts of misconduct, conversations with the other spouse that conflict with current statements, or expert testimony which bears upon custodial fitness are typical kinds of testimony that require advance preparation.

When the witness is interviewed, the lawyer prepares some form of outline of what will be testified to. Putting the testimony in sequence, noting pertinent dates when certain events occurred, and perhaps including key words that will remind the witness of the incident during the trial testimony, assist both witness and lawyer in synchronizing their presentation.

If the testimony is extensive, or if the witness is extremely nervous, the lawyer may give him a copy of the outline or a list of key questions that will be asked so he will feel more confident. Although the witness cannot use this copy to refresh his memory on the stand, the advance knowledge of what specifically will be asked builds confidence.

It is also proper to show you or your witness *how* to testify. Presuming the testimony is a hundred percent true, it may not *sound* true if presented improperly. There are do's and don'ts in the courtroom, as anywhere else, that determine the credibility and overall effect that each witness has on the outcome of your case.

See Courtroom Do's and Don'ts for You and Your Witnesses on page 113 and ask your lawyer if he has any to add. For a more detailed guide to courtroom performance, read Hints for Being a Better Witness on page 116.

CAUTION: The preparation just described is not illegal or unethical in the least. Nevertheless, time and again, when asked on cross-examination whether he has discussed this case with anyone, the witness, with the trial questions burning a hole in his pocket, will answer no. He presumes from the question that there must be something shady in discussing the testimony beforehand.

186. How do I prepare myself for trial?

Consult the following check list for questions you may want to ask your lawyer, but, in fact, there may be very little that you have to do. If you participated in the discovery proceedings and kept up to date with the negotiations, you probably know more about the case than anyone else. It is the selectivity, or narrowing down of the information to the relevant issues, that becomes crucial in presenting a good case in court.

187. What is a trial outline?

It is a script for the conduct of the case. If the case is a simple one, the outline can be kept in your head, and no written document is required. But no matter how experienced or capable the lawyer, the witnesses should know in advance what questions will be asked and what answers expected. Therefore, a pretrial interview of witnesses and outline of their testimony is important for each of the witnesses as well as the lawyer. The outline displays the case in perspective and lets the witnesses see where they fit in the total picture.

The more complicated the litigation, the more valuable the trial outline becomes. It is both an organizational tool and a check list indicating what details in terms of case preparation have been completed and what remains to be done. By having this outline

106

QUESTIONS TO ASK YOUR LAWYER BEFORE TRIAL

1. What are the main points that we are trying to prove?
2. What is my spouse trying to prove?
3. When will I testify? How long will I be on the witness stand?
4. Should I memorize anything for the trial?
5. If I get nervous and forget something important on the witness stand, how will you help me remember?
6. If the other lawyer rattles me during cross-examination, how will you help me out?
7. What should I say if he asks me —— (mention the question or questions that you have been fearing most).
8. What questions will the other lawyer probably ask me?
9. What should I bring to court?
11. Can I bring my notes to the witness stand? Can I refer to them from time to time? Can the other side look at my notes?
12. Will I be able to communicate with you when I am on the witness stand?
13. When the trial is in progress, and I am *not* on the witness stand, where will I sit in relation to you? Can I talk to you then? How should we communicate?
14. During trial recesses can I talk to you about my testimony?
15. When should my witnesses come to court? Where should they wait? Can they watch the trial *before* they testify? How about *after* they testify?
16. May I bring a friend or relative who is not going to testify, to be with me for moral support?
17. If there is a custody or visitation issue, should I bring the children to court? If so, when? where?
18. How should I dress for court?

---

available to you at various stages of the proceeding, you have a greater sense of security and awareness of the progress of your case. If a trial actually takes place, the outline enables the lawyer and his witnesses to be on the same wavelength when questions are asked.

See the sample Trial Outlines beginning on page 149.

188. What are exhibits?

Exhibits are physical evidence, in the form of letters, deeds, canceled checks, savings-account passbooks, or other documentation, which is offered in support of your case or in opposition to your spouse's case. Exhibits may also help demonstrate or illustrate points you're trying to explain. They might include photographs, floor plans, financial or other summaries.

For example, you may offer a deed with your name on it as an exhibit to prove that you, rather than your spouse, are the owner of a particular parcel of real estate. You may offer a financial statement your spouse signed to obtain a car loan, which will prove that his net worth is $50,000 rather than $25,000, as he now alleges. A chart may illustrate how the operating expenses of a closely held corporation have grown faster than sales over a period of years.

A point can be made more effectively if visual as well as verbal evidence is offered. The artful use of exhibits frequently controls the outcome of the case. Inanimate objects seem less likely to lie, though, of course, facts that are written down or diagramed are not necessarily true.

You may want to prepare a list of potential exhibits for your lawyer, indicating what facts they are intended to prove or illustrate. The lawyer will decide which are relevant and admissible as evidence.

189. What is a subpoena?

A subpoena is the court's official way of requiring an individual who is not a party to the action to testify in court or at a deposition. Some forms of subpoena require the witness to bring certain records, documents, or other tangible evidence within their control, such as bank records or photographs.

If the witness has been properly served with the subpoena and fails to appear, a contempt proceeding can then be instigated. The sheriff then can take the witness into custody and bring him before the court.

If there is a legitimate reason for not honoring a subpoena, such as poor health, the lawyer serving the subpoena should be advised. Any dispute about the legitimacy of the excuse is resolved by the judge if a contempt proceeding is commenced.

190. Can diaries or journals be subpoenaed?

In most cases they can. If you prepare certain documentation for your lawyer *specifically* for the trial or presentation of your case, it may be deemed a "work product" and be privileged against discovery, just as a private communication with your lawyer would be. However, if you look at the diary or journal on the witness stand or in the deposition, you have probably waived your privilege, and the document is subject to scrutiny and questioning by the other side. If the diaries or journals were prepared with no relation to the proceedings, they are subject to discovery.

On deposition you may be asked whether you have any diaries or other memoranda which would refresh your recollection on a given point. If you answer yes, that diary may be subject to examination unless you prepared it specifically for your attorney.

CAUTION: Check with your lawyer beforehand if you maintain a personal diary or journal that has entries that may harm your case. There is nothing illegal about disposing of such documentation *before* production has been requested. This is not true, however, regarding business records, canceled checks, and financial records. Destruction of the latter will certainly lead to claims of misrepresentation or fraud, which will hamper your case.

191. Can my diaries or journals be used as evidence if they are stolen by my spouse?

Most states hold that even if evidence is procured by an illegal search or seizure in a civil action (as opposed to a *criminal* action), it is subject to discovery and use on trial if it meets the tests of relevance and authenticity for evidence. (See Witness's Guide to the Rules of Evidence, page 144.)

That calendar on the kitchen wall where you have been noting your bowling activities five nights a week can be offered in evidence to counter your later claim that you bowled only one night a week. Before it is accepted as evidence, your spouse must be prepared to prove that the notations were made by you and that the issue of nights away from home is relevant.

192. I have letters and sworn statements from various witnesses who could not appear at the trial; may I offer these in evidence?

Probably not, unless the other side agrees to the admission of those documents. They are hearsay in nature and do not allow the other side an opportunity of cross-examination to test their truthfulness. Neither does the judge have an opportunity to observe the person who has written the letter or prepared the statement in order to make independent observations as to credibility. The hearsay objection and its exceptions is one of the most confusing and most misunderstood rules of evidence. It is defined in a simplified form in the Witness's Guide to the Rules of Evidence, page 144.

THE TRIAL

193. What are opening statements?

First the plaintiff's lawyer and then the defendant's lawyer make a brief opening statement to the judge, describing what they intend to prove. A good opening statement is a simple synopsis of the case and contains no statements that will not be later supported by evidence. The purpose of the statements is to give the judge an overview of the trial so he will appreciate the relevance of the evidence to particular issues. If there has been an extensive pretrial conference, the importance of the opening statement is diminished, and it may be waived altogether. The opening statement should not be an argument on the merits of the case to be presented.

194. Do the witnesses testify in any particular order?

That depends on the lawyer's trial outline, which he prepares in final form immediately prior to the trial. The order of witnesses is a matter of strategy and technique, with weaker, but necessary, witnesses going first and the stronger witnesses following. If there are a number of witnesses for the plaintiff's case, the plaintiff will most likely testify last, so as to fill in any blanks left by prior witnesses. If there is a particular witness whose testimony is especially powerful, that witness may be saved for last, because the lawyer will want the plaintiff's case to be finished on a high point.

195. What is the difference between direct and cross-examination?

When your lawyer questions witnesses called on your behalf, it is called direct examination. At the conclusion of the direct examination the other lawyer may question the witness further in an attempt to undermine or discredit his testimony. This is called cross-examination. Witnesses are generally cooperative and straightforward on direct examination but may be evasive or at least defensive on the cross-examination. They are aware that the examiner is trying to undermine the credibility of their testimony.

Direct examination: In conducting the direct examination the lawyer cannot put words in his witness's mouth—that is he cannot *lead* the witness. For example, a leading question would be: "On the first day of May 1979, did your husband strike you with a lead pipe about the face and body and then repeatedly kick you when you fell to the floor?" When the witness predictably answers yes, it is really the lawyer testifying and not the witness. The proper direct question would be: "What occurred between you and your husband on May 1, 1979?"

Cross-examination: On the same event, cross-examination has no such restriction. The lawyer could ask, "Is it not a fact that your husband did not strike you at all on May 1, 1979? Wasn't he defending himself while you struck *him* with a lead pipe?" That question is leading but admissible—because there is no other way to get the information on that point from a presumably hostile witness.

Preparation: You can see why it is crucial that you and your witnesses be prepared for direct examination so you can understand the import of your lawyer's *nonleading* questions and give the expected answers. It is equally important that witnesses be given some idea of what to expect on cross-examination so they aren't taken by surprise or flustered.

Binding testimony: Another difference between direct and cross-examination is that you are *bound* by the testimony of your witnesses on direct examination, even if it is harmful to your case. In other words the judge will believe the unfavorable things said by a witness who is supposed to be on your side. This is not true on

111

cross-examination or when a witness called to testify on your behalf is so evasive and uncooperative on the stand that the judge declares him or her a hostile witness.

Check the Witness's Guide to the Rules of Evidence (page 144) for a more detailed discussion of evidence problems and solutions.

196. How important is cross-examination?

Cross-examination can hurt your case if the credibility of witnesses is undermined or if they make admissions harmful to your side. On the other hand, cross-examination can help you by expanding and reinforcing the direct testimony.

The good cross-examiner does not go over *every* point that is brought out on direct testimony. Instead, he attacks only areas of direct testimony where some weakness exists, or where he hopes to achieve a particular result (a harmful admission or an incriminating silence). A cross-exam that is an aimless fishing expedition will simply reinforce the direct examination by having it repeated and unshaken. The cross-examiner who takes as much or more time than the direct examiner is often conducting an ineffective cross-examination. Another rule of thumb on cross-examination: when the answer is in doubt, it is better not to ask the question. Surprise answers from hostile witnesses usually hurt.

197. Can I turn cross-examination to my advantage and make it support my case?

Yes. Cases are sometimes won on the other side's poor cross-examination. You can prepare with your lawyer certain answers that will score points in favor of your case if you are given the right opening. By asking "what" or "why" questions on cross-examination, the lawyer frequently opens the door to new areas of testimony that could not have been covered on direct examination due to restrictive rules of evidence.

For example, on direct examination you are not permitted to tell what was said in a telephone conversation if it was hearsay. In cross-examination, when you are asked what *you* said, you can use that as an opportunity to get the entire conversation in evidence. "Why did you remove the money from the joint savings account?" might be your chance to respond, "Because when my husband's friend called on the telephone, he said [hearsay on direct examination and inadmissible] that my husband had been threatening to remove the money himself in order to purchase a car for his new girl friend." Presuming that answer to be true, and actually responsive to the question, the cross-examiner will no doubt cringe.

"What" and "why" questions open the door to all kinds of testi-

COURTROOM DO'S AND DON'TS
FOR YOU AND YOUR WITNESSES

Appearance

DO dress as you would for an important event.

DO ask your lawyer's opinion on your clothes in advance.

DON'T dress down to gain sympathy.

DON'T overdress to be impressive.

DON'T chew gum.

Courtroom behavior and courtesy

DO exercise self-control, no matter what is said.

DO be punctual for scheduled court appearances.

DO write your lawyer notes to communicate with him, or wait for a recess.

DO try to act natural.

DON'T grimace or react to answers of other witnesses or questions of the other lawyer to indicate your displeasure.

DON'T whisper in your lawyer's ear during examination of other witnesses.

DON'T engage in arguments with your spouse or opposing counsel within earshot of the judge.

DON'T be too sweet and proper, or the judge will think you phony.

Witness-stand behavior

DO your homework.

DO trust your lawyer to help you remember.

DO listen to the entire question.

DO ask to have it repeated or rephrased if you don't understand.

DO speak up—loudly enough to be heard.

DO keep your hands away from your mouth.

DO keep your voice modulated, even in the face of intimidation.

DO look the questioner squarely in the eye.

DO direct your answers to whomever is asking them —or to the judge.

DON'T memorize answers—it shows, and you may forget the exact words.

DON'T worry about forgetting.

DON'T start thinking about your answer before you have heard the whole question.

DON'T shout. DON'T mumble.

DON'T look around the courtroom while you answer, or at the court reporter, or at your spouse, or at other witnesses.

DON'T tell even small lies. If discovered, they will taint your credibility on the more significant issues.

DON'T feel the need to explain every answer: "What I mean by that is . . ." sounds evasive.

Courtroom Do's and Don'ts, continued.

DO tell the truth, even when it hurts—the judge will admire that. If the truth will destroy your case, then settle before you get to trial.

DO answer yes or no when you can.

DO ask if you can expand your answer when you cannot answer yes or no.

DO trust your lawyer to protect you by objecting to argumentative questions.

DO express an opinion *if* you are an expert on a particular question or subject and it's requested.

DO act as if the cross-examiner is your friend and you want to be helpful—which will make his job more difficult.

DON'T ask to expand every yes or no answer.

DON'T argue with the questioner.

DON'T ask questions back: "What would *you* do if . . ."

DON'T express personal opinions or conclusions unless they are specifically requested by the lawyer or judge.

DON'T be cute.

DON'T be a wise guy.

DON'T give flippant answers.

DON'T try to ingratiate yourself with opposing counsel or the judge.

DON'T be hostile or act as if your spouse's lawyer is the enemy.

DON'T try to outsmart the other lawyer—or yours either.

DON'T assume the lawyer has an ulterior motive for every question.

CAUTION: Your conduct in the courtroom or chambers may have more effect on the judge than your testimony.

mony about motives and intentions. They allow the kind of full answers that may bring out information that can be harmful to the questioner. The witness cannot be stopped as long as the answer is essentially responsive to the question. Such is the price the cross-examiner pays for a bad question.

Demeanor: Your attitude or demeanor under cross-examination can also help your case. Witnesses should assume a manner that suggests the cross-examiner is their friend and they want to be helpful (as far from the truth as that may be). Otherwise, a skillful cross-examiner can undermine the credibility of a truthful witness merely by provoking hostility. If you let the cross-examiner get under your skin, you are far more likely to display a darker side of your character and weaken your case. If the other lawyer believes the direct testimony to be essentially accurate, he may deliberately

DO be straightforward.

DO answer even those questions that appear insulting or stupid, unless your lawyer objects.

DO ask permission of the judge to not answer a specific question—and give the valid reason (for example, that the answer will endanger someone or unnecessarily jeopardize someone's reputation).

DO answer the question if the judge then instructs you to (or you can be found in contempt).

DO use language most comfortable and natural to you.

DO tell the story accurately if you are complaining of violent, abusive language that your spouse uses in front of you or the children.

DO say yes if asked whether you have discussed the case with a witness, or whether the witness has discussed the case with you or your lawyer.

DO answer a simple yes or no to a tricky question: for example, "Would you have this court believe that . . ."

DON'T act defensive or suspicious on cross-examination, by your look or tone of voice.

DON'T refuse to answer any question unless you have a valid reason.

DON'T use language that is formal or unnatural—it detracts from your credibility.

DON'T be, or pretend to be, too shy or modest to quote the exact words your spouse used when being abusive or vulgar.

DON'T add unnecessary comments—"And I can prove it!" or "And that's the truth!"—which sound as if everything else you said was unprovable or a lie.

try a few upsetting questions (usually personal or in an accusing tone) just to provoke a hostile reaction and thus reveal the witness as less amiable than he or she seemed on direct examination. Refuse to take the bait: display instead an attitude of cooperation. The lawyer will probably quickly terminate his cross-examination. If he plods on, your answers will only reinforce the direct examination and might gain sympathy or respect on the part of the judge if the questioner is obnoxious.

HINTS FOR BEING A BETTER WITNESS

WHEN YOUR LAWYER IS QUESTIONING YOU
(Direct Examination):

1. Appearance: The first impression you will make on the court is by your physical appearance. Don't dress down for court to gain sympathy. Don't overdress to be impressive. Dress as you would for any important event, such as a job interview or a luncheon with a wealthy relative from whom you hope to inherit. Don't be afraid to ask your lawyer his opinion on your intended clothes for court. Look good!

2. Courtesy: Be punctual for scheduled court appearances. Do not chew gum in court. Do not exhibit hostility or rudeness toward your spouse or your spouse's attorney, no matter how you may feel about them. Assume an attitude when answering questions that you are attempting to be helpful, without appearing overeager. The judge will have an opportunity from time to time to observe your conduct in court, and your courtesy will make an impression. Judges like nice people, but don't overdo it. Acting like a goody-two-shoes will make you appear phony.

3. Preparation: If you have done your homework with your attorney before court you will be less nervous, and the court will appreciate your preparation. A prepared witness does not have to *memorize* answers. If you are telling the truth and have the overall outline of your case in mind, your attorney will make sure that any forgotten points are covered. That's his job, so don't you worry about it. If you have carefully thought through the events about which you will testify, you should be able to visualize them at trial, and no memorization will be necessary. If there are lists of items that are involved in your testimony, your attorney can prepare exhibits in advance containing these lists, which you can verify on the witness stand. A witness is expected to be nervous and is expected to forget things. Witnesses who have memorized testimony can usually be spotted immediately by the glassy haze in their eyes as they attempt to recite. Unfortunately, any interruption, especially on cross-examination, may upset the whole train of recollection, and the witness may collapse altogether. Memorizing also causes you to worry about forgetting—and worry makes you forget.

4. Listening: When you are asked a question on the witness stand, don't be thinking about your answer until the question is completed. Listen to the question in its entirety. If you do not understand it, ask to have it repeated or rephrased. Lawyers often ask questions that are too wordy or have too many compound clauses, not because they are trying to be tricky, but because they are not sure of what they want to ask. Most lawyers do not write out their questions in advance, so they are thinking as they go. Unfortunately, the mouth often moves faster than the brain, and you need not struggle with the muddled result. Just say, "Could you repeat the question, please?" or "I don't understand the question." The court will know if it's a bad question and so will the lawyer. If he has to frequently repeat or rephrase his questions because they are muddled, he'll become more nervous than you are, and the judge will be irritated with the questioner—not with you.

5. *Volume:* Speak up, but don't shout. Keep your hands away from your mouth when you speak and don't mumble. Your lawyer should adjust your volume as you answer the first few questions put to you, either by asking you to keep your voice up or by moving farther away from you in the courtroom, which has a tendency to increase the witness's volume. Some lawyers on cross-examination have a tendency to shout at the witness in order to be dramatic or intimidating. Should this happen to you, do not shout back. Shouting is an irritation to the court and induces sympathy for the witness. The attorney will likely be reprimanded for his conduct. In the meantime, your carefully modulated responses in the face of such intimidation will make a positive impression on your behalf. Direct the answers to questions to the attorney who is asking them, or to the judge if the judge is asking them. Do not be looking around the courtroom when you answer, or at the court reporter, or at your spouse, or at other witnesses. Looking the questioner squarely in the eye gives an impression of truthfulness, sincerity, and all sorts of good things.

6. *Truthfulness:* The keystone of effective testimony is truth— even when it hurts. If the truth will destroy your case, then settle. The lying witness makes a very bad impression on the court, and the results of your case can be seriously affected. Even little white lies can convey the impression of overall untruthfulness and taint the more significant issues. If there are any areas where you fear to tell the truth, make sure to go over them with your attorney in advance. He can assist you in answering these questions with the least amount of damage, but still without your having to tell a falsehood. Ironically, the court sees so much lying that a witness who is particularly candid in response to difficult questions may earn the admiration of the court and be rewarded in the ultimate outcome of the suit.

7. *Responsiveness:* Be direct in your answers to questions. Answer yes or no when you can. Beating around the bush makes you sound as if you are lying even when you are telling the truth. If the question cannot be accurately answered yes or no, then say so. The

Hints for Being a Better Witness, continued.

court will give you an opportunity to expand on your answer. If you repeatedly seek the opportunity to expand on your answer, however, and if in the majority of instances it appears that you could have answered the questions yes or no, you will undermine the effectiveness of your testimony by apparent evasiveness. It is amazing how witnesses can succinctly answer yes or no to questions on direct examination, but then slip into a defensive shell on cross-examination and insist on giving extensive answers to simple questions. The overall effect is the appearance of untruthfulness.

8. Language: Use the phrasing that is most comfortable to you when you are on the witness stand. Language that appears too formal or in any way unnatural to you detracts from the credibility of your testimony. This also means that you should "tell it like it is." If you're complaining about the violent, abusive language that your spouse uses toward you or in front of the children, don't pretend you're too shy to quote the exact words that were used. Your testimony will be more memorable and more credible where you quote exactly.

9. Opinions: If you have expertise in a certain area, you may give expert opinions after a proper foundation has been laid. As a layman you may also give opinions under certain circumstances where you have personal knowledge of the underlying facts. However, you should avoid spicing your testimony with your personal opinions and conclusions unless they are specifically requested by the attorney or the court. Not only do you violate the rules of evidence when you give an opinion without a proper foundation, but if you do it frequently, you may give the impression of being officious or arrogant. It is the court's duty to render opinions on the evidence. Your layman's opinion will be requested only where necessary to aid the court in understanding the evidence.

10. Argumentativeness: Don't argue with the questioner or ask questions back. For example, if asked "What did you do after such and such happened?" don't answer "Well, what would you do?" If asked "Did the children visit their father last Sunday?" don't answer "Well, would you let your children visit someone who has been drinking all afternoon?" Just say no. If the lawyer wants to follow up with a "why?" you can then give him both barrels. If the attorney has been argumentative in the manner of his questions, your attorney will protect you with an objection. Questions like "Were you lying then or are you lying now?" or "Why didn't you take proper care of your children?" are argumentative and objectionable.

11. Acting out: You're as much on trial when you are off the witness stand as when you are on. Don't grimace or shake your head or otherwise react to the answers of other witnesses on the stand or to the questions being propounded by the other attorney. This kind of playacting inevitably makes a bad impression on the court. It is distracting and has an air of false self-righteousness about it. The court will form its own opinion as to the truthfulness of the witnesses without help from the peanut gallery. Self-control is not always easy, but it will make you look better than constant upstaging of the witness.

WHEN YOUR SPOUSE'S LAWYER IS QUESTIONING YOU
(Cross-Examination):

12. Review: Read over hints 1 through 11—they all apply on cross-examination.

13. Conduct: Even though you may believe your spouse's attorney is the enemy, pretend that he is not. Don't be hostile; don't be cute; don't be a wise guy; and by all means, don't try to outsmart the other lawyer. The more hostile the witness, the easier the cross-examination, because that hostility can be exploited by the attorney. Don't try to guess the ulterior motives to his questions, because very often there may be no such motive. A flippant or evasive answer will only serve to give a bad impression—exactly what the attorney wants you to do. Very often, on cross-examination there are no particular facts that can be disputed from your direct examination. Ground may still be gained by the skillful cross-examiner if you can be provoked into appearing temperamental, stubborn, biased, or evasive. If you can just psych yourself into a frame of mind whereby the cross-examiner is your friend and you wish to be helpful, you will make his job extremely difficult.

14. Refusal: Often questions on cross-examination may appear to you to be insulting or stupid. Answer the question anyhow, if you are able. The judge will sense the stupidity of the question and admire your patience. Don't *you* object to questions, even if they are objectionable. That is your attorney's job, and very often he may not make objections for a strategic purpose. At this point you must rely on him and not take matters into your own hands. If a question is asked that you do not wish to answer for a valid reason, like unnecessary injury to a third party's reputation, ask permission not to answer the question, stating the reason. If the judge still instructs you to answer the question, do so. Refusal can result in a finding of contempt, or at least give the impression that you're hiding the truth.

Hints for Being a Better Witness, continued.

15. *Defensiveness:* Most witnesses tend to be defensive on cross-examination because they are suspicious of the motives of the questioner. The witness most often displays a defensive attitude by evasiveness, hostility, or outright lying. The clever cross-examiner will take advantage of these tendencies by phrasing questions that are argumentative or loaded with presumptions. The best remedy, combined with your determination to be "helpful," is to answer the questions simply, directly, and truthfully. For example, many questions will be opened with the phrase "Would you have this court believe that . . . ?" Right off the bat there is the presumption in the question that you are not to be believed, and the tendency is to argue back. Instead, just answer yes or no and see how devastating the effect can be. "Would you have this court believe that you never struck your wife?" "Would you have this court believe that at no time did you remove monies from your joint savings account and give them to your girl friend for safekeeping?" "Would you have this court believe that you never abandoned your children in order to be with your lover?" To all of these questions, answer a simple yes if that is the case. If the answer is no, then the attorney must ask additional questions to find out what it is that you *would* have the court believe. At this point you give him both barrels of your factual shotgun.

Another common ploy is to ask whether a witness has discussed the case with the party for whom he is testifying, or the party's attorney. The answer, obviously, should be yes, but the defensive witness will often be evasive or tell an outright lie. There are many forms of questions that tend to encourage your natural tendency to be defensive, but they are, in reality, a form of trick question recognized by the court, and it is the manner of your answer as much as the substance that will give an overall positive or negative impression. The real danger for the cross-examiner is that if the questions are answered well, the cross-examination enhances the direct examination rather than undermines it. The skilled cross-examiner will terminate his examination when he discovers he is failing to undermine the credibility or composure of the witness.

16. *Overspeak:* Another symptom of defensiveness on cross-

examination is the tendency of witnesses to gratuitously add unnecessary comments to their testimony. When you finish up a question with "And I can prove it," or "And that's the truth," or "And I have witnesses," you are not underscoring the truthfulness of your statement. You are merely suggesting that the rest of your testimony was not truthful, or you were not able to prove it, or not supported by witnesses. When Lily Tomlin, the comedienne, does her routine with the little girl on the big chair, her most outlandish statements are followed up with the famous phrase "And that's the truth." The humorous irony, of course, is the fact that the statement is obviously exaggerated or untrue. Avoid these gratuitous phrases, which have a tendency to give an impression opposite to the one of credibility that you intended.

17. Opening the door: A basic rule for the cross-examining attorney is to never ask a question if he is not fairly certain of what the answer is going to be. For that reason, questions that begin with "how" or "why" are always fraught with danger. They open the door for the witness to come forth with seemingly endless self-serving testimony to explain how or why something was done or said. A well-prepared witness will look for these openings in order to get evidence in the record that was not admissible on direct examination because of restrictive rules of evidence. For example, where you are unable to get the content of a conversation with a third party in evidence on your direct testimony because of hearsay, a "what was said" question to any part of the conversation on cross-examination may open the door for the entire conversation going into evidence. Attorneys frequently lose their case on cross-examination by inadvertently opening the door to areas of testimony that were not otherwise admissible, thereby making the case for the other side. Once the door has been opened, it cannot be shut as long as your answer is responsive to the question. The seemingly innocuous "Why did you leave the house that evening?" may well cause the attorney to cringe at the five-minute response reciting the fears that the witness was experiencing at the vicious conduct of the drunken spouse whose girl friend had called on the telephone several times that evening and said that she was having an affair, etc., etc., etc.

Fortunately for you, most lawyers are not the devastating cross-examiners we see portrayed in movies and television. A reasonably poised witness who is telling the truth will find cross-examination less difficult than direct examination, and the resulting testimony will carry greater weight because it is brought out by the other side.

For a more detailed discussion see the Witness's Guide to the Rules of Evidence, page 144.

198. What is an affirmative defense?

In addition to showing why the allegations of the other side are untrue, the defendant's case may bring forth new facts or legal defenses. For example, in fault states, proof of provocation may be a legal defense to an allegation of marital misconduct. ("He *made* me do it.")

An *affirmative defense* is a direct attack on the plaintiff's case which, by presenting proof of new factual matter, *legally* bars the plaintiff from the relief sought.

199. What is "counter-relief" in the defendant's case?

If the defendant in addition to answering the complaint, asks for relief such as custody, child support, alimony, division of personal property or real estate, the defendant will then have to present evidence in support of those counter-claims.

200. Should I be concerned if at the trial my lawyer presents our defense differently from the way we had prepared it?

Probably not. A good trial lawyer should be sufficiently flexible to adjust the defense to the evidence presented by the plaintiff as well as to the attitudes of the trial judge. Sensing the judge's attitudes as the case develops is part of the art of trying a case.

For example, the reactions of the judge to particular witnesses or evidence presented can determine what evidence should be emphasized to satisfy *this particular judge*. If the judge appears to be a strict moralist, you may emphasize marital misconduct as an affirmative defense, hoping to gain sympathy on your behalf. Another judge might be offended or bored by this type of evidence, in which case it is better to play it down or omit it from your defense altogether.

CAUTION: The selection of the trial judge may substantially predetermine the outcome of the case because of the known predilections of that judge. Even if you are right as far as the law and the facts are concerned, you may lose the case because the judge was more concerned with evidence that appealed to his particular prejudices. Judges have a great deal of discretion in their interpretation of the facts as they apply to the law in a divorce case. This broad discretion makes appeals based on the judge's interpretation of the facts very difficult to win.

201. Does the completion of the defendant's case end the trial?

No. The plaintiff has the opportunity for rebuttal—to present additional evidence to rebut any *new facts* brought to light in the course of the defendant's presentation. To the extent that the defendant's case merely denies or conflicts with the evidence presented by the plaintiff, no rebuttal is necessary.

Surrebuttal is merely the defendant's opportunity at the end of the rebuttal testimony to present evidence in relation to any *new matter* that was raised in the rebuttal. This part of the trial usually goes rather quickly because the judge, in most cases, has already made up his mind and has little patience with additional testimony. If you find that he is hurrying the lawyers along in their examinations or sustaining virtually all objections, you can be fairly certain that his decision has been made.

202. What does "off the record" mean?

When a shorthand reporter is making a transcript of the trial, the judge and even the lawyers may ask to go "off the record" in order to make a statement that should not properly be considered by the judge in the conduct of the trial. For example, "What time will we be breaking for lunch today, Your Honor?" is clearly a comment that belongs off the record.

A problem sometimes arises when the trial judge or the opposing lawyer makes frequent comments off the record that may affect the conduct of your case and should therefore be *on the record*. A comment by the judge, for example, about a particular witness or particular evidence that was presented should be on the record because it may affect testimony if the comment is made within a witness's hearing. The comment may also reflect some error or bias in the judge's thinking, which will be grounds for appeal. A judge does not like lawyers to insist that comments be made on the record when he has already prefaced his statement with "off the record," and lawyers don't want to anger the judge unnecessarily. Nevertheless, if the judge regularly makes prejudicial comments off the record, it may be necessary to insist they be on the record in order to preserve the record for an appeal.

203. What is a mistrial?

A mistrial occurs when an error is committed that is serious enough that it makes a fair trial impossible. If that happens, one or both of the lawyers, or the judge himself, makes a motion for mistrial. The proceedings are terminated and reassigned to another judge to begin again. Granting or refusing a motion for mistrial is a matter of the judge's discretion.

204. Why are there so many conferences in chambers with the judge and lawyers during the trial?

In most cases the chamber conferences are an informal method of exchanging information between the judge and the lawyers to expedite the trial. Typical topics are the order of the witnesses, the anticipated length of testimony, evidence problems, or the hour at which the trial will recess or resume. Judges sometimes get bored hearing a particular case, and the in-chamber conference is in fact a break or social gathering between judge and lawyers at which the case is not discussed at all. This is not a bad idea if the judge's concentration would lag otherwise.

Litigants often become anxious about frequent communications with the judge that are conducted out of their hearing, but they have no reason for concern if both lawyers are present. Most trial judges are sensitive to the litigant's apprehension, and to avoid any suggestion of impropriety will not see either lawyer alone during the conduct of a trial.

205. What are closing arguments?

They are the statements by the respective lawyers summarizing the evidence that has been presented during the trial. Because they are "advocates," each lawyer attempts to argue or slant the evidence most favorably toward his own client. Misstatements of the evidence are not permitted, but the judge has taken notes during the trial and presumably disregards emotional excesses or inaccuracies.

206. Is there any point, then, in making a closing argument if the judge has already made up his mind?

Unlike jurors at jury trials, judges are not very likely to be swayed by the closing arguments of the lawyers. Judges are trained and experienced in dealing with complex factual situations and should be able to ferret out the relevant testimony as it is presented in order to come to a conclusion by the time the evidence is completed. However, when a trial is complicated, or has continued over an extended period of time, or involves unique questions of law, the lawyer should insist on his right to a closing argument.

124

A good closing argument will be more factual than dramatic. The lawyer selects the evidence that is most supportive of his case, as well as the evidence that is most detrimental to the opponent's case. When questions of law are involved, the lawyer may argue *particular facts* as they relate to the law or lead to a certain legal conclusion.

In a long trial, certain bits and pieces of evidence may not seem significant at the time they are presented, but become increasingly important as the entire case unfolds. One can never be sure whether the trial judge has remembered that small piece of evidence or omitted it from his notes. The trial judge is more likely to be persuaded by a factual argument that assists him in *organizing* the evidence to a logical conclusion than by an argument that is emotional. A closing argument that takes on the aspects of a harangue may be more detrimental than helpful to the overall case.

Clients frequently feel cheated if their lawyer does not make a closing argument, because that is one aspect of trial highly emphasized in the entertainment media. For that reason, the closing argument may be more for the client's benefit than for the judge's.

207. When does the judge rule?

The judge will rule either at the conclusion of the trial or a short time thereafter if he indicates the matter is being taken "under advisement." The latter phrase indicates that he wishes to review the evidence before making a final decision. If the judge rules immediately at the end of the trial, without reviewing the evidence, it does not necessarily mean that he has not considered all of the evidence.

Most trial judges at the conclusion of the hearing try to find something in their ruling for both of the parties. Most trial judges prefer that both parties go away a little bit happy—as difficult as that may be. The trial judge is likely not to see the evidence in the blacks and whites that the adversaries do, and therefore makes his ruling in shades of gray. Various compromises may be implicit in the ruling without the judge's actually knowing the client's true priorities.

208. How does the judge's ruling relate to the final decree?

The last step in the trial process is the drafting and entry of the decree or judgment. The lawyer incorporates the judge's ruling into the decree in the same manner in which he would have incorporated the parties' oral agreement, had a settlement been reached without trial. A copy of the drafted decree is usually given to opposing counsel in advance for approval. After any disputes have been worked out over the form or substance of the provisions, the decree is presented to the court for entry.

If the lawyers cannot agree on certain provisions in the decree, each may submit his own decree for entry and the judge can decide which version is proper. The lawyers may conduct an oral argument before the judge in support of their particular version of the final decree. The judge can also draft his own decree in place of what the lawyers have submitted.

209. What if I don't accept the judge's ruling?

If either party strenuously objects to the court's judgment, a motion to vacate the decree, or a petition for rehearing or to present new evidence may be filed within term time, which in most states is thirty days from the entry of the decree. If the motion is denied, or if the lawyer determines that nothing can be gained by making such a motion, he may proceed to file an appeal to a higher court.

210. What are the chances of an appeal's success?

More often than not, when the appeal is based on the trial judge's *interpretation* of the evidence, the appeal will fail. Trial judges are given broad discretion in interpreting evidence because they have the advantage of observing the witnesses as they testify, while the appellate judges can only read the testimony. However, if the trial court's ruling is contrary to what the evidence obviously proved (manifest weight), then the appellate court will reverse for "an abuse of discretion."

If, on the other hand, the trial judge has committed some legal or procedural error which has substantially affected the outcome of the case, the chances of the appeal's succeeding are far greater.

Because the cost of an appeal may exceed that of trying the case in a lower court, and because the time consumed in the appellate process may be a year or more, the parties in divorce cases are frequently better off accepting even a bad judgment if they can live with it, rather than prolonging the agony through appeal.

211. Does my divorce lawyer handle the appeal if I want one?

Yes, or he will assist you in finding appellate counsel. In either case, the fees and costs of the appeal will be in addition to what you originally agreed upon for handling the negotiation and trial. Some lawyers never handle appeals and others specialize in appellate work.

WRAP-UP

212. When is my divorce decree effective?

You are divorced; the support is to be paid; and the property to be transferred when the judge signs (enters) the decree, unless its specific provisions say otherwise. In some states the original decree is *interlocutory*, which means that a prescribed period of time must pass before a final judgment is entered and before the parties may remarry. Your lawyer will advise if your decree is interlocutory.

Note: Decrees are interlocutory only in the states of: California (6 months); Nebraska (6 months); Massachusetts (6 months); Utah (3 months).

213. What happens after the decree for divorce has been entered?

Your lawyer will follow it up by completing the various items called for in the decree, whether it is entered by agreement or after contested trial. This involves the transferring of real estate and personal property, the revising of wills, the modification of insurance policies, and other details that are necessary to complete

127

the physical separation of the parties and the transfer of their property.

See the Windup Check List (page 132) for a summary of the details that may have to be completed before your case is terminated.

214. What Social Security, retirement, or disability benefits is a divorced spouse entitled to?

Until recently a divorced spouse could not get benefits on the former spouse's earnings record unless the spouse had been contributing to his or her support following the divorce or under a court order to do so. *That support requirement has been eliminated.* For example, a woman who had been denied benefits in the past solely because of this requirement should reapply for benefits immediately. Currently, the former wife of a man who is getting retirement or disability benefits is entitled to a benefit on *his* record if she is at least sixty-two years old and had been married to him for at least *ten years* before the divorce.

215. How about Social Security survivor's benefits?

A divorced wife is entitled to survivor's benefits after the death of her former husband if she is at least sixty years old (fifty if disabled) and was married to her former husband at least ten years before the divorce; or if she is caring for a child who is either under eighteen or disabled and who is getting benefits on the same record. The child must be her natural or legally adopted son or daughter. Generally, a divorced wife must be unmarried at the time that she applies for benefits. The rules on remarriage of divorced wives are the same as those for widows, with one exception: the special provision for widows who remarry at age sixty or later does not apply to divorced wives.

216. May I change my name?

Yes. A name change can be part of your divorce decree upon request. You can also do it later, but there may be additional costs and attorney's fees. Many mothers choose not to revert to a maiden name in order to save their children the complication of explaining a different name. In most states, you can use whatever name you wish as long as the purpose is not to defraud.

For further information you may write:

Center for a Woman's Own Name
261 Kimberly
Barrington, IL 60010
(312) 381-2113

217. Is a spouse required to give back stolen papers used in the divorce?

Yes, if it can be clearly established who owns the papers. Documents which have been marked as exhibits and accepted in evidence may have to remain in the possession of the court until the possibility of appeal has ended. After that period (usually thirty days following the final judgment) each spouse is entitled to his or her own papers and personal effects. Unfortunately, when the parties remain bitter toward each other these personal items tend to mysteriously disappear.

218. How are modifications made in my divorce decree?

If the modification is by agreement with your former spouse, a court order can be filed detailing the change.

If you don't agree, a petition for modification must be filed, detailing whatever change in circumstances makes this change necessary. Basically, the only modifiable areas of a final divorce judgment relate to the children and certain types of alimony provisions. The court will conduct a hearing on the contested modification after notice to the objecting spouse, and a court order will be entered granting or denying the relief requested.

219. Is there a time period during which my divorce agreement cannot be modified?

Child-support payments are generally modifiable upon proof of a substantial change in the children's need, or of a substantial change in the payor's financial ability to pay. The latest child-support order was based on the needs of the children and respective financial abilities of the parents *at that time*. Some support orders contain ranges of income where support increases are prohibited or automatically provided for. Courts will generally honor such arrangements, but *can* alter them where the children's welfare requires it.

Alimony payments that are not limited as to time or amount are generally modifiable on the same basis as child support, and end upon death of either party or remarriage of the recipient. In the case of alimony—unlike that of child support—the parties can agree in their written settlement that alimony installments are fixed as to the number of installments and the amount, and can *prohibit* the court from modifying their alimony agreement. Under some settlements alimony installments may even continue at the same or a lesser rate for a specified period after remarriage—these are called "prodder" provisions, which encourage remarriage.

Unallocated (combined) alimony and child-support payments

are more complicated in terms of modifiability. Some courts do not accept modification limitations in a written settlement agreement insofar as they attempt to limit child support. However, interpretations are constantly changing in the various states and even in courts within a state. Consult your lawyer whenever you are considering an unallocated support settlement and again when modification is sought, because the law may have changed. The tax benefits of unallocated support agreements make them worthwhile even if their modifiability is uncertain.

Property divisions, whether imposed by the court or agreed to by the parties, are not modifiable unless the agreement has some provision for modification based on future contingencies. For example, the wife may be given the residence outright, but the husband will receive a portion of the sale proceeds if she remarries within a specified number of years.

220. Is a husband liable for payment of alimony if his wife is living with another man (or vice versa)?

Living together in the same residence for a continuing period of time causes termination of alimony in those states that have adopted some form of the Uniform Marriage and Dissolution of Marriage Act. In other states, cohabitation may be a basis for terminating or modifying alimony only if the person one is living with provides money for the household, thus reducing the former spouse's need. Either way, the relationship must be one of a continuing nature. Modification or termination of alimony is not intended as a punishment for misconduct.

221. What if my spouse doesn't comply with the provisions of the decree, or with any court order?

The court retains jurisdiction over the parties and their children to enforce its orders, judgments, and decrees. A variety of enforcement procedures is available, including garnishment of wages or bank accounts, seizure of property, and imprisonment or fines for willful contempt of court. If your former spouse isn't complying, your lawyer should be promptly consulted for the appropriate time and method for solving the problem. If in your community child support is enforced through the Friend of the Court or state's attorney, he should be consulted (see Question 65).

222. Who pays for enforcement or modification proceedings?

The spouse in willful violation of a court order may be assessed lawyer's fees and court costs, but ultimately the one who pays will usually be decided on the basis of financial ability.

The same is true of modifications. Don't be surprised if you have to pay fees even if your spouse is the wrongdoer. The lawyer can't be expected to work for free and if *you* can't collect from your spouse, your lawyer is sure to have the same problem. If enforcement is available through the Friend of the Court or state's attorney, no fee is normally charged to the party seeking enforcement.

223. Are alimony payments taxable?

Yes. Periodic payment for the support of a spouse (as opposed to property division) are taxable to the recipient and deductible to the payor for federal income-tax purposes if the following conditions are met:

1. The parties must live in separate households when the payments are made;
2. The support obligation must be set forth in a court order or judgment, or a written agreement signed by the parties (not their attorneys);
3. The payments must be either:
   (a) Installments payable over an indefinite period of time (e.g., until death or remarriage); or
   (b) Installments payable over a definite period of time which exceeds ten years; or
   (c) Installments payable for a definite period of time less than ten years, but subject to earlier termination upon the happening of a contingency such as death or remarriage.
4. Child-support payments are not tax-deductible unless they are combined with the alimony payment without allocation as to how much is either child support or alimony. If the conditions of paragraphs 1, 2, and 3 are met, the unallocated payment of alimony and child support is then deductible in its entirety by the payor and taxable in its entirety to the recipient.

Whether or not your alimony payments are subject to state taxation is a matter of individual state law, and your accountant or attorney should be consulted.

Since the current trend is to structure divorce settlements around the tax laws, your attorney should advise you during the course of negotiations and upon entry of final judgment as to the tax effect of any support payments. You should record any support payments paid or received in a calendar year in a notebook in order to prepare an accurate tax return. You may also have to file quarterly estimated income-tax returns if you are the recipient of taxable support. Have your attorney or accountant assist you in planning for your first alimony-affected tax return; you can probably prepare your own returns thereafter.

224. Are property transfers incident to a divorce taxable?

The general rule is that the increased value of property transferred between spouses as part of a divorce is taxable as a capital gain to the party making the transfer. If, for example, a husband transfers title to the marital home or stock to his wife as part of the divorce, and that property is worth more now than when he bought it, 40 percent of the gain is added to his ordinary income and taxed.

There are so many exceptions and qualifications to this rule that your tax adviser must be consulted as to the taxability of particular divorce transfers. There is now pending in Congress the Domestic Relations Tax Reform Act of 1983, which is intended to simplify this complex area of law. Among other things, this act will provide that transfers of property to a spouse incident to dissolution will be treated in the same manner as a gift. There would be no tax to the party making the transfer, but there would be a tax on any gain in value over the original cost when the transferee later sells or transfers the property. Your attorney will have to advise you as to this and other proposed changes if this legislation passes.

225. Is inherited property attachable?

Yes. It is subject to satisfying indebtedness or arrearages established by court orders or judgments, the same as any other property. Inherited property has special significance only at the time of division of marital or community property and is generally not included as part of the divison.

226. When is my lawyer's representation of me completed?

When the necessary documents are exchanged or recorded, your lawyer closes your file, and his representation is completed. Should matters of enforcement or modification of the decree arise at a later time, those are generally considered to be new legal matters, and if the same lawyer is retained, new financial arrangements must be made with him.

In most states, notice of a post-decree petition to modify or enforce must be served on the *other spouse* rather than the other lawyer if more than thirty days have passed since the final decree or order was entered. Use the Windup Check List (p. 134) to see that all details are being completed *as soon as* your decree is entered. If there are any errors or misunderstandings in connection with the decree, try to get them resolved or at least in court for resolution within the thirty-day period. That way you will save additional fees and potential jurisdictional problems.

227. Does the entry of the final decree terminate my relationship with my ex-spouse?

Not if you have minor children or if the decree requires a continuing financial relationship between you. Both the welfare of your children and your own peace of mind make it imperative that you and your spouse come to some form of truce. You are not expected to be lovers, or even friends, but why continue the acrimony that probably causes extreme distress to both of you? Your psychological divorce will never be complete as long as you are vindictive toward each other. New marriages or relationships will be jeopardized by lingering bitterness, and noncompliance with the decree's provisions will provide the artillery for a continuing legal war.

WINDUP CHECK LIST (Closing Your File)

When your final decree has been entered, there will be documents to be prepared by the attorneys and executed by the parties. Some of the documents will have to be recorded and others merely delivered to the other attorney or spouse. The following check list will help you make sure that no detail has been overlooked. The initials after each item indicate the type of windup activity that may be required to complete your file. Check items that apply to your case (√):

   (P)repare   (E)xecute   (R)ecord   (D)eliver

1. *Real estate*
   New deeds or assignments (P, E, D, R). Existing deeds, title insurance or abstracts, bills of sale, plats of survey, buyer/seller closing statements, appraisals, leases (D); assignment of leases (E, D); homeowners, renters, owner/landlord/tenant insurance policies (D). Assign beneficial interest to spouse retaining property.

2. *Vehicles*
   Automobiles, boats, airplanes, trailers, motorcycles, or other vehicles (E, D, R). Confirm insurance coverage and assign beneficial interest to spouse retaining property.

3. *Securities*
   Stock certificates and bonds (E, D, R); assignments separate from stock certificate or bond (P, E, D, R); bearer bonds (D).

4. *Insurance*
   a. Policies of life insurance: ( ) conform beneficiary designations as per decree; ( ) furnish proof of policy maintenance; ( ) consider furnishing insurer with copy of decree if insurance borrowing or modification are restricted; ( ) furnish copy of policy.
   b. Policies of health insurance: ( ) conform beneficiary designations as per decree; ( ) furnish proof of policy maintenance; ( ) furnish beneficiary I.D. card; ( ) furnish copy of policy or schedule of coverage; ( ) furnish conversion documents *immediately* if spouse is converting group policy to individual coverage (there may be a thirty-day limit).
   c. Homeowner, tenants, automobile or business insurance: ( ) conform beneficiary designations to decree and ( ) deliver policies as required.

5. *Debts*
   (   ) Inventory balances due creditors as of decree date.
   a. Household expenses: (   ) compute the amount due from each spouse on debts to be divided pro rata as of a certain date; (   ) change billing on utilities or charge accounts; (   ) close charge accounts which are to be terminated; (   ) get final billings; (   ) surrender or destroy charge cards as per decree. (   ) Advise creditors who rendered credit jointly in the past of your nonliability for future debts of spouse. (   ) Furnish statements in your possession for accounts to be paid by other spouse; (   ) obtain statements in spouse's possession for accounts to be paid by you.
   b. Loans from third parties: (   ) obtain releases from creditors, if possible, where other spouse is assuming the debt; (   ) obtain written indemnification and hold-harmless from spouse for debts assumed by him or her if not contained in the decree; (   ) change billing address if necessary; (   ) deliver payment booklet, promissory note, mortgage, or other documentation to party assuming debt; (   ) consider letter to creditor advising of spouse's assumption of liability and requesting notice in event of default prior to institution of any collection procedures.
   c. Debts between spouses: (   ) P (   ) E (   ) D, any notes to be exchanged between spouses as part of property settlement; (   ) verify that any security devices (to guarantee specified payments) called for under decree have been executed or effectuated as required, e.g., lien on real estate or maintenance of life insurance in amount equal to unpaid balance of lump-sum settlement to be paid in future installments.

6. *Bank accounts, C.D.'s, etc.*
   a. Savings-account passbooks: (   ) D, conform account ownership to decree; (   ) verify balance as per decree or agreement; (   ) consider reinvestment for higher yield.
   b. Certificates of deposit: (   ) D, conform account ownership with decree.
   c. Treasury bills and notes: (   ) D, conform ownership with decree.
   d. Checking accounts: (   ) D, canceled checks and bank statements; (   ) conform account title with decree; (   ) close or remove name from accounts that spouse could overdraft.
   e. Money-market accounts: (   ) conform account ownership with decree and (   ) D.

7. *Income tax*
   (   ) Verify whether joint return is to be filed with spouse, dis-

Windup Check List, continued.

position of refund or liability; who is to prepare return; ( ) D, supporting income and deduction documentation. ( ) Obtain hold-harmless and indemnification for tax liability in past years if appropriate. ( ) Clarify tax liability for exchanges of property under divorce decree, year of declaration and possible exemption or deferral of tax. (   ) Clarify tax liability from alimony or periodic payments; ( ) arrange for tax reserve in proper amount and filling of quarterly estimates.

8. *Estate planning*

( ) Consult with attorney regarding necessity of will; ( ) revise estate plan if appropriate and consider investment advice as to any assets from marital settlement not needed for current living expenses. ( ) Depending on size and complexity of estate, an attorney, accountant, or financial consultant may be advisable to set you on the right financial track from the outset of the divorce.

9. *Trusts*

Assignments of beneficial interest or powers of direction for existing trusts ( ) P; ( ) E; ( ) D. New trust agreements to secure alimony, child support, educational needs or some testamentary purpose ( ) P; E; ( ) D.

10. *Personal-property exchange*

Household furnishings, personal effects, tools, jewelry ( ). Arrange time and place for pickup or delivery.

QUESTIONS TO ASK YOUR LAWYER UPON
ENTRY OF THE FINAL DECREE

When your case has been completed and your final decree entered, you still have to record deeds, deliver documents and property, and pay monies due. The following questions should give you perspective on what to expect in your new divorced status and assist the windup of your file.

1. When is my decree for divorce, separate maintenance, or annulment final or effective? When will I receive a copy of the decree?
2. When can I remarry?
3. When are support payments due? How should I keep track of the payments and how should they be allocated as to alimony or child support?
4. What documents should I receive from transfers of real estate, vehicles, securities, insurance policies, and the like? What documents am I to execute? Who will prepare these documents? Who will record them?
5. What is the balance of my attorney's fees and costs? Are there any additional fees or cost charges in connection with the windup of the case?
6. When should I expect other personal property, such as furniture, to be picked up or delivered? Who is responsible for delivery arrangements and costs?
7. If my spouse is not complying with the decree in the matter of support payments or delivery of property or documents, what should I do?
8. Who will pay the attorney's fees and court costs in connection with any enforcement proceedings?
9. Now that I am divorced, should I have a will or should my present will be revised?
10. Can I file a joint income-tax return for this year? What records should I keep for income tax in future years?
11. Can I take the children out of town for vacations?
12. Can my girl or boy friend come along on visitation?
13. How will a live-in girl or boy friend affect custody rights?

CHECK LISTS, SCHEDULES, AND GUIDES

INITIAL INTERVIEW INFORMATION SHEET

Personal background
1. Names and addresses of spouses.
2. Maiden name of wife.
3. Dates and places of birth of spouses.
4. Religions of spouses.
5. Residence phones of spouses.
6. Business phones of spouses.
7. Personal health of spouses, with details of any extraordinary physical or psychological problems.
8. Educational background of spouses and special training, if any.
9. Date and place of marriage to current spouse and number of prior marriages and how terminated.
10. Address to which mail should be directed, if not the residence address, and telephone numbers where client may be contacted, if not the residence or work phone number.

Children
11. The names and birth dates of each child of this marriage, indicating any child who is deceased or of age, and whether or not the wife is pregnant. Also, the address of any minor child who is not residing

at home, and the name of the person with whom the child is residing.

12. The names and addresses of any persons, other than the parents, who may claim a custodial right to the children.
13. The names and ages of any children of the spouses by a prior marriage and the name and address of the person who has their custody.
14. Any financial obligations to children of a prior marriage.
15. Any special needs or disabilities of any of the children.
16. The school status of the children and the quality of their performance.
17. Any agreed upon or contemplated custodial arrangement and visitation arrangement by the noncustodial parent.
18. Any facts or circumstances that cause you serious concern about your spouse's acting as custodian or exercising rights of visitation.
19. Children's career or educational goals, if known.

Income and property

20. The occupation and business address of each spouse.
21. The gross salary of each spouse. The take-home pay and whether each spouse receives a commission or income from some other source, with identification of the source.
22. Whether the spouses have been filing joint income-tax returns, and whether either of them files returns other than personal returns, such as partnership or corporate returns.
23. Whether either party is contemplating an employment change in the foreseeable future, and how that will affect their income.
24. The employability of a spouse, if unemployed.
25. A description of any checking and savings accounts maintained by the parties, the balances contained therein, the named titleholders to the accounts, and the source of deposits.
26. A description of any securities owned by the parties, current market value, named titleholder, date of purchase, and source of purchase money.
27. Location of any stock certificates and whether any substantial sales have been made in preceding months.
28. A description of any real estate owned by the parties, purchase price, current market value, mortgage balance, monthly payments, including taxes and insurance, date of purchase, source of purchase money, and your preference regarding disposition of particular parcels of real estate.
29. A list of personal property, including household furnishings, automobiles and other vehicles, boats and jewelry; valuations where available and desired disposition.
30. A description of any safe-deposit boxes maintained by the spouses and the contents thereof.
31. A description of any insurance policies maintained by the spouses. The beneficiaries and the death benefits of life insurance. Name of any health and accident insurer.

140

32. A description of any monies due either spouse and a list of outstanding debts other than monthly utilities.
33. A description of any gifts or inheritance that are anticipated by either spouse or their children.
34. Any financial obligations to a spouse of a former marriage.

Specific marital problems

35. A description of the cause and duration of any marital separations during the entire marriage period.
36. The spouses' history of marital counseling, if any.
37. The spouses' history of psychological counseling, if caused by other than domestic problems.
38. The last occurrence of sexual relations between the parties and whether there had been any significant change in the frequency of sexual relations over the preceding months.
39. Whether the client feels that any aspect of the parties' sexual relationship has led to their present estrangement.
40. Whether either of the spouses has previously filed suit for divorce or separate maintenance, or consulted lawyers in connection with problems of this marriage.
41. What discussions, if any, the parties have had about separation or divorce.
42. The actions or omissions of the other spouse that cause the client to seek legal advice at this time.
43. What alternatives, if any, the parties have considered or discussed other than separation or divorce.
44. The specific conduct of the other spouse that would constitute grounds for divorce, such as the irretrievable breakdown of the marriage, incompatibility, cruelty, or marital misconduct.

Relief requested

45. The current financial needs of the parties and their children, in the form of a budget and any change in those needs contemplated in the near future.
46. The client's expectations and preferences regarding the division of property in the event of a divorce.
47. The immediate needs of the client in terms of support, housing, debt assistance, injunctive relief, physical protection, or custody and support of the children.
48. Whether or not either spouse has long-range support needs.
49. The intentions of the parties regarding remarriage and employment.
50. The present plans of either party to relocate their residence.
51. Whether the wife wishes to resume her maiden name in the event of divorce.
52. Whether there are problems in the home, between the spouses or with the children, that require immediate attention through professional counseling.

CHILD-SUPPORT SCHEDULES—SAMPLES

I

Child Support Alone

Number of Children	Percent of Husband's Income (Net)
1	20%
2	27%
3	35%
4	42%
5	50%
6	55%
7 or more	55%

As indicated previously, the support allowance determined under the basic formula should be adjusted upward or downward to reflect other relevant circumstances.

II

Child Support and Maintenance

Number of Children	Percent of Husband's Income (Net)
1	35%
2	40%
3	40%
4	45%
5	50%
6 or more	55%

The breakdown as to how much of the total allowance should be considered child support and how much should be considered maintenance would be left to the discretion of the judge. "Wife" should be substituted for "husband" wherever the latter term appears, if the wife is the noncustodial parent.

III

Maintenance Alone

No guidelines will be considered where there are no minor children and the only question before us is maintenance. In these cases the great variety of fact situations makes it impractical to attempt to use a formula. The amount of maintenance may vary from nothing to 50% of the income of the spouse from whom maintenance is sought.

The statutory presumption *against* maintenance places the burden on the party seeking it to show that they are unable to support themselves satisfactorily.

(Schedule continued on next page.)

GUIDELINES FOR TEMPORARY SUPPORT ORDERS
SAN FRANCISCO BAY AREA SUPERIOR COURTS

NET MONTHLY INCOME[1]	SPOUSE ALONE[2]	SPOUSE & 1 CHILD	SPOUSE & 2 CHILDREN	SPOUSE & 3 CHILDREN	CHILD SUPPORT[3][4] ONLY (per child)
$ 400	$100	$ 100	$ 100	$ 100	$ 50-$ 75
500	200	200	200	200	75- 100
600	250	300	300	300	75- 100
700	300	350	375	400	75- 100
800	325	400	425	450	100- 125
900	375	450	475	500	100- 125
1000	400	500	550	600	100- 150
1200	475	600	650	700	100- 150
1400	550	700	800	850	125- 175
1600	650	800	900	950	125- 175
1800	750	900	1000	1050	150- 250
2000	800	1000	1100	1150	150- 250
Above 2000	40%	(and court will exercise discretion re child support)			

[1] Of noncustodial parent for child support; of one spouse for spousal support of the other. Income considered "net" after compulsory deductions such as income tax, FICA, and any standard deductions which are for the benefit of the family, but not including deductions for credit union obligations or savings, or other payroll savings plans. The schedule assumes the supported spouse will have no income-tax obligations on the amounts ordered.

[2] Where both spouses are employed, if one's income is 60% or more of the other's, no spousal support; if less than 60%, one half of the supported spouse's net earnings (after child care expenses) should be deducted from this figure to determine the guideline for temporary spousal support. Other columns would be adjusted.

[3] If there are more than three children, such amount per child as reasonable under the circumstances (not by multiplying the number of children by the figure in the last column).

[4] The figures in this column are based upon the assumption that the net earnings of the custodial parent are not more than 75% of the earnings of the noncustodial parent and that there is no award of temporary spousal support.

If the noncustodial parent carries hospital, medical or dental insurance covering the children, the guideline figures may be reduced by any cost attributable to the children's coverage.

143

WITNESS'S GUIDE TO THE RULES OF EVIDENCE

The rules of evidence that control the conduct of court hearings and, to a lesser degree, depositions, are extremely complex and vary slightly from state to state. The following simplified guide is designed to give you an overview so that you at least have some idea what is going on at your deposition or trial. Once you get a feeling for these rules, don't be upset if your lawyer doesn't object to every leading question or hearsay answer. Good trial technique suggests that the attorney object only to what may damage your case and not to every harmless error. The hearing will pass much more quickly as a result, and you will avoid irritating the judge with needless objections.

1. Purpose: While laymen often object to the apparent strait jacket that the rules of evidence put on their testimony, the actual purpose of the rules is to provide a system for speedy and fair trials. The rules require evidence to be presented in a manner best designed to determine the truth.

2. Burden of proof: The spouse who is seeking any particular relief from the court has the obligation of pleading allegations which justify that relief and then coming forward with testimony or other evidence that will persuade the court that his or her allegations are more probably true than not. If you fail to sustain your burden of proof on an issue, the court finds against you. You lose.

3. Character evidence: Inevitably, people in divorce or custody litigation want to bring their friends and relatives to testify as character witnesses. As a general rule, character evidence is not admissible in divorce proceedings to prove that a spouse did or did not engage in a particular course of conduct. Neither is it admissible to prove that John is a "good guy" and Mary is a "bad guy," so John should win. Where a witness's reputation for truthfulness has been attacked, some jurisdictions do allow a limited type of character testimony as to the witness's prior reputation for truthfulness or untruthfulness. This type of testimony is rarely seen in divorce court.

4. Personal knowledge: As a general rule, witnesses other than experts testify from their own knowledge—their personal observations. Opinions or interpretations of what you observed will not be required, or allowed, in most cases. The judge will render his own opinion on the evidence in making his final determination.

5. Expert witnesses: Individuals who have specialized knowledge about some factual issue involved in your lawsuit may testify to assist the court in understanding the evidence and reaching a final determination. Experts may testify from personal observation, from data examined before the trial, from facts presented at the trial, and from their special knowledge and training. Psychologists, psychiatrists, appraisers, economists, and social workers are some of the experts who are frequently called to testify in matrimonial cases. While they will testify as to their expert opinion on an issue, the court only considers that opinion with the other evidence and is not bound to accept it.

6. *Foundation:* Before certain evidence will be accepted by the court, a preliminary "foundation" must be established. For example, the foundation for a conversation will require preliminary evidence as to when and where the conversation took place, and who was present. The foundation for a photograph will require testimony from a person familiar with the scene or object being photographed, indicating when the photograph was taken and whether it is a fair and accurate representation of the scene being photographed. The purpose of the various foundation requirements is to assure the court that the evidence being offered is true and accurate.

7. *Refreshing recollection:* When a witness is testifying and has exhausted his memory regarding a particular event or transaction, the witness may refer to a written document to refresh his recollection. Having inspected the document, he then resumes testifying. If the document is a memorandum that was made by the witness at the time of a particular occurrence and records details of the occurrence, it may be admitted in evidence if the witness's recollection is incomplete. If the document was made later on, or was not prepared by the witness, it may only be used to refresh an exhausted memory. Documents and lists prepared for trial may be used in this manner, but once they are used, they are subject to examination by the other side and may be referred to on cross-examination. Your use of documents to refresh your recollection on the witness stand should be arranged with your attorney beforehand as part of your trial preparation. You don't sneak a peek at these documents, you refer to them only with the permission of the court.

8. *Objections:* Where rules of evidence are being violated, this fact is called to the attention of the court by either counsel, who makes an objection to the question being asked or the answer given. The court also has the right to make objections, but the witness may *never* make an objection. If the objection is to the question, the attorney waits until the question is completed and then orally makes his objection and states the reason for it. The court will either sustain (allow) the objection or overrule it. In the latter case, the witness then proceeds to answer the question. If the particulars of the question have been forgotten, the witness may ask the court reporter or the attorney to repeat it. If a question has been asked and answered without objection, then any possible objection is waived and the testimony becomes part of the record. The following is a summary of the most common objections that you are likely to hear.

OBJECTIONS TO THE FORM OF THE QUESTIONS:

A. *Leading:* On direct examination, the questioner should not suggest the answer in the question, with the result that the witness need only answer "yes" or "no." Instead of saying "Did you deposit $10,000 in your joint savings account on January 15, 1980?" the questioner should ask whether the witness deposited any money in the savings account, when, and how much. That way the witness is testifying and not the lawyer, and the court is able to measure the credibility of the witness. In order to save time it is generally acceptable to ask leading questions on preliminary information and to assist a witness who has exhausted his recollection. Leading questions in crucial factual areas will not be allowed if objection is made. Of course, once a leading question has been made and objected to, it is a simple matter for the attorney to rephrase his question in proper form, and the witness will know the information being sought. If this is done repeatedly, the questioner may be reprimanded by the court. In any event, the credibility of the testimony will be undermined if a witness is constantly led.

B. *Compound question:* A question containing two or more questions is confusing to the witness, and any attempted answer may confuse the court. The attorney should ask only one question at a time. The same is true of questions that are ambiguous or not clearly phrased. If an objection is made, the court will ask counsel to rephrase the question.

C. *Lack of foundation:* If the questioner seeks to elicit certain testimony or the admission of documentary evidence that requires a preliminary foundation, the court will sustain an objection to its admission until the foundation is properly laid by the required series of questions.

D. *Presumption of facts not in evidence:* Where the questioner includes in his question facts or presumptions that are not in evidence or that are in dispute, the question is objectionable. "When did you first start beating your wife?" or "What did you do to stop your wife's overspending?" are objectionable unless the beating or overspending are undisputed. The answer will be confusing because it will not be clear whether the witness is admitting the presumed facts. This type of manipulative question will frequently confuse or anger the witness who is not able to catch the presumption and correct it before answering the rest of the question. The same is true where the questioner misquotes the witness's testimony on direct examination in a cross-examination question. The question should be objected to and the quotation corrected before any answer is given. You should be wary of any cross-examination questions which tend to put words in your mouth, especially if the words taste unfamiliar.

E. *Argumentative:* Questions that are intended to persuade the judge rather than elicit information, or that call for an argument from the witness, are objectionable. The questioner frequently tips off his argumentative implication by beginning the question with a phrase like "In other words" or "Would you have this court believe?" If the argumentative question is not objected to, the witness is better off answering "yes" or "no," if that is possible, rather than arguing back.

F. *Repetitive:* The witness need not answer the same question over and over again, even if the form of the question is slightly changed each time. One answer on each point is enough, and repetition is usually done on cross-examination for purposes of harassment or to elicit slight differences in the multiple answers so as to create discrepancies that may undermine the witness's credibility.

146

OBJECTIONS TO ANSWERS:

A. Unresponsive: If the witness's answer goes off the subject of the question, the questioner can object to the answer as being unresponsive and ask that the answer be stricken from the record.

B. Narrative answers: On direct examination, questions should be specific. If the question is so broad it requires a long narrative answer, the opposing attorney will not be able to anticipate objectionable testimony. Once the inadmissible testimony has been spoken, the objection may well be too late. Therefore, the attorney has the right to object to broad questions before they are answered. The question "Can you tell us how your husband treated you last year?" is too broad, and if objection is made, the court will require the attorney to rephrase the question, directing it to some particular conduct or particular time that is relevant to the subject in issue.

C. Opinion and speculation: Where the witness is interpreting the evidence by giving his own opinions or speculation, the answer may be stricken from the record. Neither can the witness *characterize* conduct by calling it "wonderful," "negligent," "good," "evil" or by using other adjectives that inject editorial opinion into the events being described.

OBJECTIONS TO CONTENT OF QUESTION OR ANSWER:

A. Irrelevant: Evidence is relevant if it tends to prove or disprove some matter that is at issue in your case. If it is not relevant, the court does not want to hear it because it does not aid in the determination of the case. In matrimonial cases, clients have a tendency to want to litigate many issues that ventilate their feelings as to who is the "good guy" and who is the "bad guy" in their marriage, and they are disappointed when the court refuses to admit such testimony. The primary difference between a skilled lawyer and a layman in matters of litigation is a trained sense of relevancy. What is emotionally most important to you may be irrelevant to the court.

B. Hearsay: You cannot testify to the verbal or written statement someone made, unless your spouse was present. This is one of the most widely known—and widely misunderstood—rules of evidence because of its many exceptions. For your purposes as a witness, it is enough to know that you or your witnesses cannot testify about what Betty, John, or Bob said if your spouse was not present to hear it. The reason for the rule is the lack of opportunity to cross-examine Betty, John, or Bob to determine whether they really made the alleged statement and whether what they said was true. On the other hand, if in preparing for trial, you have evidence that may appear to be hearsay, don't discard it. Call it to your attorney's attention, and you may find that it is not hearsay after all, or that it is admissible as an exception. It is also not a bad idea to prepare certain hearsay testimony; though it may not be admissible on your direct examination, it may be sprung on the opposition in response to a careless question on cross-examination.

C. Exceed scope of direct examination: The cross-examiner raises questions relative only to the subject matter contained in the direct

147

testimony and cannot bring up new matter unless it is done in the attempt to undermine the credibility of the witness. If the cross-examiner seeks to open new areas of inquiry with the witness, he must wait and recall the witness when he puts on his own case.

TRIAL OUTLINE: GROUNDS (FAULT STATES ONLY)—SAMPLE

I. *Introduction*
   A. Name, address, age, length of residence in the jurisdiction.
   B. Date and place of marriage; number of children born or adopted to this marriage; children by prior marriages living in home.
   C. Employment of witness and spouse.

II. *Conduct of witness as a spouse*
   A. Activities as homemaker or breadwinner, or both.
   B. Contribution toward child care.
   C. Any other evidence that witness was a dutiful spouse.

III. *Grounds—misconduct of other spouse*
   A. *Option 1:* Relate events *chronologically,* for example:
      1. Late Dec. 1968: Relate physical-cruelty act that required medical treatment.
      2. 1970–1979: Relate series of lesser acts, including physical and mental cruelty, that have more significance as a *course* of cruel conduct, presuming no single act is of great magnitude, e.g., pushing, shaking, poking with finger, some of which is done in front of friends, along with vile or abusive language, so as to cause humiliation. Add evidence of other misconduct, such as increasing lack of affection, staying out late at night without explanation, dissipation of income and assets, nagging, unjustified criticism, etc., as they occurred in a given time period.
   B. *Option 2:* Relate events *categorically,* for example:
      1. Relate all acts of physical cruelty from 1968 to present.
      2. Relate all examples of belittling or demeaning conduct in front of third parties from 1968 to present.
      3. Relate examples of late hours, lack of affection, etc., from 1968 to present.
   C. *Option 3:* Combine categorical and chronological, for example:
      1. Relate physical and mental cruelty by category during 1968 to next significant time period, e.g., 1974, when the youngest child entered school.
      2. Relate acts of physical and mental cruelty by category from 1972 to next significant time period, then to present.
   D. After relating events, detail conduct or event that led to final separation. It is best if evidence leads to an apparent crisis so that a continuation of the marriage relationship appears impossible, or at least unreasonable:
      1. Add testimony that plaintiff did not cause or provoke any of the misconduct by the spouse (if necessary to counter-defense of provocation).
      2. Add testimony that plaintiff has lived separate and apart as a single person without fault.

149

E. Note in preparing your trial outline:
   1. Each incident or category of misconduct should be given a separate subheading, number, or letter so that your attorney can select those incidents that have most impact as evidence and eliminate irrelevant or minor evidence that may water down the overall presentation. Selected incidents may be moved around in the outline for more effective presentation.
   2. The most is not always the best. You may want to include *everything* in your outline, not realizing that some incidents make you look worse than your spouse. Let your attorney determine the strategy and select the events that will lead to the most effective presentation of your case.
   3. The stronger your grounds, the shorter your outline, for example:
      a. On January first we were married.
      b. On January second he hit me with a hammer.
      c. On January third he stabbed me with a sword.
      d. We separated on January third and have remained apart.
      e. I did not provoke the bludgeoning or stabbing.
         End of outline—end of case.

Unfortunately—or fortunately—everyone can't have such a strong case. The outline, in any case, is a useful tool—both to teach you what is relevant and to familiarize your attorney with the facts of your particular case. It puts you both on the same wavelength for the trial. Trial judges appreciate thorough preparation and lose patience with both witnesses and attorneys who appear not to have organized and rehearsed their presentations.

TRIAL OUTLINE: PROPERTY AND SUPPORT—SAMPLE

I. *Introduction*

Name, address, years of marriage, number of children, present employment of self and spouse (may be omitted if the judge is already aware of this information from earlier hearings on this case).

II. *Income of Spouses*

A. Present evidence of current gross income and take-home pay of self and spouse, if you know.

B. Note any improper or excessive deductions, e.g., has five children but claims no exemptions.

C. Note any trends in employment history of self or spouse, e.g., steady increase or decline; sudden decline coinciding with filing of divorce suit; opportunity for additional income from tips, expense-account overtime or bonus; incidence of unrecorded income from cash payments, moonlighting, or payment in kind, e.g., spouse does mechanic's bookkeeping in exchange for car repair.

D. Note employment benefits and "executive compensation," e.g., free insurance, use of country club, automobile, air transportation, paid vacations.

E. Note any deferred benefits from employers, e.g., pension or profit-sharing plans, bonuses, delayed salary increase, deferred commissions.

III. *Property of Spouses*

A. List all property of spouses, with valuations (if agreed). Disputed items will require present market-value testimony from a qualified witness or appraiser.

B. Property list prepared in writing in advance of trial in balance-sheet or similar form should be presented to opposing counsel for comment as to accuracy. Trial can be limited to disputed items, with a list of agreed property items offered in evidence by agreement.

C. In community or equitable-division jurisdictions, community or marital property should be separated from individual property. The latter is generally not subject to division by the court, but may affect the amount of the marital estate each spouse is awarded. For disputed items evidence must provide:

1. Time and source of original acquisition.
2. History of any transfers, tracing original asset to its present form.
3. Any prior agreements of spouses as to disposition.
4. Statement as to whether there was any commingling of title or ownership between spouses.
5. Financial contribution to acquisition and maintenance of property, including contribution as a homemaker.

151

D. In common-law property states evidence must prove:
1. Title to property.
2. Special equities from prior agreements or financial contribution.

IV. *Need of spouse and children for support*
   A. Establish family's standard of living through past activities and expenditures.
   B. Establish current living costs by written budget, which may be in affidavit form (see Living-Expense Budget, page 162), indicating both actual and estimated monthly expenses. If amounts come from check book summary, standard of living may be established at the same time.
   C. Any special needs anticipated in the near future should also be presented to the court so that they can be worked into current budget, e.g., eyeglasses, orthodontia, monthly payments on a new car, furnace, roof, etc.
   D. If other spouse is in the habit of making substantial expenditures for such things as clothing, club memberships, sports equipment, entertainment, this may be offered as proof of both a high standard of living and financial ability beyond apparent means.

V. *Advise court how special needs require a particular division of marital property: e.g., home and furniture for children, savings needed for business capital, car needed to get to work.*

VI. *Other problems or support issues.*

152

TRIAL OUTLINE: CHILD CUSTODY—SAMPLE

The following trial outline is designed for the parties themselves or witnesses who are going to describe their personal observations regarding custody issues. This outline is not for *expert* witnesses.

I. *Identification and background*
   A. Age; education; employment.
   B. Relationship to child; opportunity to observe child or parents, or both.

II. *Description of each child*
   A. Age; mental and physical health; elaborate on any special problems.
   B. Progress in school; grades; best and worst subjects; teacher comments (report cards); absenteeism and tardiness; school activities; awards; discipline; elaborate on any special achievements or problems.
   C. Child's relationship with others:
      1. Siblings (effects of separating children).
      2. Playmates (general sociability, special friends; effect of change of environment; ability to make new friends).
      3. Adults (response to authority; teachers, coaches; relatives; neighbors).
      4. Parents or parent figures (affection shown to and from child in relation to each; responsiveness to discipline; comments, complaints or expressed preference of child toward each; nature and regularity of activities with each).

III. *Physical description of present or future home*
   A. Residence: Rooms; bedroom for child; furnishings; cleanliness; other household members. Is this where child will live?
   B. Neighborhood: Physical condition of homes; proximity of friends, parks, transportation, school; incidence of crime, or other negative or positive factors.

IV. *Description of each parent or potential custodian*
   A. Witness's relationship to parent (if witness is not the parent).
   B. Each parent's background, e.g., age, mental and physical health, education, employment (history of employment can be included if it demonstrates instability or special training, etc.).
   C. Parents' past relationship with child in terms of nurturing, disciplining, regular activities.
   D. Any significant changes in a parent's relationship with child in terms of nature of activities or time spent with child.
   E. Factors that favor *either* parent as potential custodian, e.g., education, training or experience; priorities as they affect children; stability of personality, environment, or career; past history as principal nurturing parent; certainty, predictability, or

153

discernibility of future environment and conduct, as they may affect children; personal commitment to children's welfare; ability to provide alternate supervision or home care when necessary; availability of supportive family and friends to provide secure home atmosphere.

F. Factors that undermine either parent's fitness as potential custodian:

1. Prior misconduct or bad habits that have actual or potential effect on children's moral, emotional, or physical welfare.

2. Demonstrated inability to meet children's everyday nurturing needs, e.g., cooking, cleaning, affection, discipline, willingness or ability to be there when children need something or to provide suitable alternate supervision and home care.

3. Statements or conduct that suggests children's welfare is secondary priority, e.g., statements or threats in part that suggest that custody effort has ulterior motive, such as spite, leverage on other issues, or a *need* for the children, rather than the reverse; a demonstrated willingness to frequently leave the children alone or with others in order to voluntarily pursue activities that are personally gratifying; repeated attempts to involve children in marital problems, e.g., pressing for their support, efforts to belittle or downgrade the other parent in children's eyes; past indifference to necessary professional checkups or treatment for children; a dramatic change in attitude toward children from indifference to fixation that coincides with the matrimonial litigation.

4. Demonstrated or diagnosed mental or emotional illness or instability that is likely to affect parenting ability.

V. *Conclusion*

A. Witness's opinion as to custodial arrangement that will serve children's best welfare and reasons for that opinion. (In some jurisdictions only an expert witness can be asked for such an opinion.)

B. Based on witness's observation and knowledge, what harm would witness foresee if children were placed with the other parent?

SAMPLE WORKSHEETS

ASSET/LIABILITY WORKSHEET

(Provide requested information on separate worksheets in columns under indicated Roman numerals and headings.)

I. Real Estate

Address and Description	Date Acquired	Cost	Value as of (date)	Balance of Mortgage	Titleholder	Use

II. Savings, C.D.'s, Money market, Treasury bills or notes, Commercial paper

Describe Account	Date Acquired	High Balance	Source of Investment	Balance as of (date)

III. Checking

Describe Account	Date Acquired	Balance as of (date)	Average Balance	Titleholder	Used By

IV. Stocks and bonds

Name & Number of Shares	Exchange	Date Acquired	Titleholder	Value as of (date)	Cost	Where Located

V. Closely held corporations

Name and Number or Percent of Ownership	Date Acquired	Titleholder	Date & Amount of Last Sale or Valuation	Avg. Annual Income/Loss

VI. Partnerships/Joint ventures

Name & Percent of Ownership	Date Acquired	Amount of Investment	Value as of (date)	Add'l. Capital Required	Title

VII. Sole Proprietorships

Nature of Business Activity	Date Acquired	Market Value	Avg. Annual Income/Loss

VIII. Pension and Profit-sharing

Name of Plan	Owner of Interest	Date entered Plan	Vesting Date or Vested Percent	Time & Method of Distrbtn.	Value as of (date)

IX. Cash-value life insurance (Whole Life)

Insurance Company	Policy Number	Insured	Beneficiary	Owner	Value as of (date)	Loans	Annual Premium

X. Patents, Copyrights, Royalties

Owner	Description of Interest	Date Acquired	Benefits to Date	Value as of (date)

XI. Vehicles and Boats

Description	Date Acquired	Titleholder	Cost	Value as of (date)	Loan Balance

XII. Furnishings, Antiques, Artworks, Collections

(List household furnishings and appliances by room on schedule to be attached. Other items of value list below.)

Description	Date Acquired	Who Acquired	Cost	Source of Payment	Value as of (date)	Where Located

XIII. Accounts Receivable

Payable To	Name of Debtor	Balance Due	Manner & Amt. of Payments	Nature of Debt

XIV. Miscellaneous Assets

Describe	Date Acquired	By Whom	Cost	Source of Payment	Value as of (date)	Other Considerations

159

LIABILITIES

XV. *Secured debts and delinquent real estate taxes or assessments*

Creditor	Date and Loan No.	Debtor	Balance as of (date)	Monthly Payments	Describe security and name of any co-signer

XVI. *Unsecured debts and income taxes due*

Creditor	Date Incurred	By Whom	Balance as of (date)	Monthly Payment

XVII. *Contingent debts*

Creditor	Basis for Claim	When Debt Accrued	Date & Amount Due	Describe Contingencies

INSURANCE WORKSHEET

Locate all policies if possible and list them below.

I. Life Insurance:

Insurer and Policy Number   Term or Whole Life   Insured   Owner   Beneficiary   Premium   Death Benefit   Loans   Net Cash Value

II. Home or renter's insurance: (Fire, Liability, and Extended Coverage)

Insurer and Policy Number   Expiration Date   Premium   Named Insured   Agent's Phone No.

III. Auto or boat:

Insurer and Policy Number   Expiration Date   Premium   Named Insured   Vehicles Covered   Agent's Phone No.

IV. Health, accident, or major medical:

Insurer and Policy Number   Expiration Date   Persons Covered   Premium   Claims Procedure   Agent's Phone No.

V. Other insurance:

Company and Policy Number   Type of Insurance   Expiration Date   Premium   Beneficiary

LIVING-EXPENSE BUDGET

Average Monthly Expense for Maintaining Household

RESIDENCE, RENT OR MORTGAGE
PAYMENT, TAXES AND
INSURANCE

UTILITIES:
  Heat, Fuel
  Water
  Electricity
  Gas
  Telephone
  Refuse Disposal

LAUNDRY, CLEANING
MAINTENANCE:
  Maid/sitters
  Yard
  Repair and Decorating

FOOD (Meat, Groceries, Milk):

AUTOMOBILE:
  (Gas & Oil) Repairs
  License & Insurance

PERSONAL:
  Clothing
  Grooming
  Medical: Doctor
           Dentist
           Drugs
  Insurance—Life, Hospital

MISCELLANEOUS:
  Clubs
  Social Obligations
  Gifts
  Donations
  Newspapers/Magazines
  Vacation
  Installment Accounts
  (Detail on reverse)

CHILDREN: Number
  Clothing
  Grooming
  Education: Books,
  Tuition
  School Activities
  Transportation
  Lunch
  Medical: Doctor
           Dental
           Drugs
  Insurance
  Personal Allowance
  Gifts, Donations
  Books, Magazines
  Theater, Clubs
  Summer Camp

$ _____

Total $ _____

GLOSSARY

The words below are defined as they are most commonly used in connection with divorce cases.

ACTION (Same as Cause of Action.) The legal term for what is commonly called a lawsuit.

AFFIDAVIT A written statement of facts made under oath and signed before a notary public or other officer who has authority to administer oaths.

AFFIRMATIVE DEFENSE New facts or legal defenses in response to the spouse's pleading constitute a legal defense, even if the allegations of the complaint were true; a bar to legal relief.

AGREEMENT The oral or written resolution of disputed issues that is incorporated into a court order, judgment, or decree.

ALIMONY Spousal support. Same as maintenance.

ALLEGATION Statement of facts contained in a pleading, setting forth what the pleader intends to prove.

APPEAL The process whereby a higher court reviews the proceedings in a lower court and determines whether there was reversible error. If so, the appellate court amends the judgment or remands the case to the lower court for a new trial.

APPEARANCE The formal submission by a defendant to the jurisdiction of the court after having been served a summons or knowing that the complaint has been filed. Appearance also refers to the physical presence of a party at a court hearing.

BIFURCATION The trial of a case in two parts. In the first part the question of grounds for divorce is heard. If the grounds are established, the second part consists of the trial on issues involving property division, alimony, child support, custody, or attorneys' fees.

CHANGE OF VENUE A change of judges before whom the case is to be tried, requested by a party to the action who feels that the original judge is prejudiced.

CLAIM A charge by one spouse against the other.

COMMUNITY PROPERTY All income and property (regardless of who holds title) acquired by the spouses during the course of their marriage, with the exception of property acquired by inheritance or gift. The manner of division differs among community-property states, but the tendency is toward equal division. (See *joint property*.)

163

COMPLAINT   The initial pleading in an action for divorce, separate maintenance, or annulment, setting forth the allegations upon which the requested relief is based. Called a petition in some states.

CONDONATION   The misconduct of a spouse is no longer grounds for divorce if the complaining party appears to forgive it by, for example, continuing to cohabit with the offender.

CONTEMPT OF COURT   The willful failure to comply with a court order, judgment, or decree by a party to the action. Also, any willful act by a person, whether or not a party to the action, which interferes with the court proceeding or somehow contravenes the authority or dignity of the court. Contempt of Court is punishable by fine or imprisonment.

CONTESTED CASE   Any case where the court must decide one or more issues that are not agreed to by the parties. All cases are considered contested until all issues have been agreed to.

COUNT   A statement of facts in a pleading constituting the pleader's case or cause of action. A pleading may contain one or more counts: e.g., a count for divorce and a count for legal separation. In some cases the counts are pleaded separately, and in others they are combined.

COUNTER-CLAIM   A pleading filed by the defendant, making claims against the plaintiff.

COURT ORDER   The court's written ruling. See *order*.

CROSS-EXAMINATION   The questioning of a witness presented by the opposing party on trial or at a deposition. The purpose is to test the truth of that testimony or to develop it further.

DECREE   The final ruling of the judge on an action for divorce, legal separation, or annulment. Same as judgment.

DEFAULT ORDER OR DEFAULT JUDGMENT   An order or judgment given by the court without the other side's being heard because they failed to plead within the time allowed or failed to appear at the hearing.

DEFENDANT   The one who defends the lawsuit brought by another. Same as respondent.

DEPOSITION   The testimony of a witness taken out of court under oath and reduced to writing. The most common depositions are discovery depositions taken for the purpose of discovering the facts upon which a party's claim is based or discovering the substance of a witness's testimony prior to trial. The deposition may be used to discredit a witness if he changes his testimony. Evidence depositions are used to preserve the testimony of a witness who will be unable to appear at trial.

DIRECT EXAMINATION   The initial questioning of a witness by the attorney who called him to the stand.

DISCOVERY   Procedures followed by attorneys in order to determine the nature, scope, and credibility of the opposing party's claim. Discovery procedures include depositions, written interrogatories, and notices to produce various documentation relating to issues which are decided in the case. Psychological examinations and court social-service investigations are also part of discovery.

DISCRETION OF THE COURT   The area of choice available to a judge to make a legally acceptable decision on *his* interpretation of the evidence.

EMANCIPATION   The point at which a minor child comes of age. Children are emancipated in most states upon reaching the age of either eighteen or twenty-one, or upon marriage, full-time employment or entering the armed services. Emancipation terminates the duty to support unless a state's statutes require support for the disabled or for educational purposes, i.e., high school or college.

EQUITABLE DIVISION OF PROPERTY   A system of dividing property acquired by spouses during their marriage in connection with a divorce proceeding. The division is based on a variety of equitable factors, including relative financial contribution; contribution as a homemaker and respective need. Title to property in the name of either spouse does not necessarily restrict the court's right to award that property to the other spouse as part of an equitable division.

EVIDENCE   Documents, testimony, or other demonstrative material offered to the court to prove or disprove allegations in the pleadings.

EX PARTE   The application for court relief without the presence of the other party, due either to a lack of notice or the choice of the other party not to appear.

FOUNDATION   The evidence that must be presented before asking certain questions or offering documentary evidence on trial. See the Witness's Guide to the Rules of Evidence, page 144.

GROUNDS FOR DIVORCE   The legal circumstances which must be proved before a divorce can be granted. Only Illinois and South Dakota currently require proof of marital misconduct. The other states require proof of either incompatability, irretrievable breakdown of the marriage or separation for a specified minimum period.

HEARING   Any proceeding before the court where testimony is taken or arguments offered by the attorneys for the purpose of resolving disputed issues.

HOLD-HARMLESS   When one spouse assumes liability for a debt or obligation and promises to protect the other from any loss or expense in connection therewith.

HOSTILE WITNESS   A witness who demonstrates so much prejudice during direct examination that the party who has called him is allowed to cross-examine. The greater flexibility of cross examination enables the questioner to ask leading questions and to attack the creditability of the hostile witness. See the Witness's Guide to the Rules of Evidence, page 144.

IMPEACHMENT   The act of proving either by prior inconsistent statement or other conflicting evidence that a witness is lying.

INDEMNIFICATION   To promise to reimburse another person in case of an anticipated loss; the same as hold-harmless.

INJUNCTION   A court order forbidding someone from doing a particular act which is likely to cause physical or mental injury or property loss to another party.

INTERLOCUTORY DECREE   A judgment of the court that is not final until the passage of a certain period of time. During the interlocutory period the parties cannot remarry.

INTERROGATORIES   A series of written questions served upon the opposing party in order to discover certain facts regarding the disputed issues in a matrimonial proceeding. The answers to interrogatories must be under oath and filed within a prescribed period of time.

JOINT PROPERTY   Property held in the name of more than one person. (See *community property* and *marital property*.)

JUDGMENT   The order of the court on a disputed issue; same as decree.

JURISDICTION   The power of the court to rule upon issues relating to the parties, their children or their property.

LEGAL SEPARATION   A cause of action for support while the spouses are living separate and apart; in many states this is called separate maintenance. Actions for legal separation provide for maintenance, child custody, and support, but generally do not provide for division of property. A decree of legal separation does not dissolve the marriage and does not allow the parties to remarry.

LEVERAGE FACTORS   Particular considerations, based on the priorities of the parties, which induce them to settle disputed issues. The skillful employment of these leverage factors generally controls the successful outcome of a settlement.

LUMP-SUM ALIMONY   Spousal support in a single payment or fixed total sum paid in periodic installments. Sometimes called alimony in gross.

MAINTENANCE   Spousal support; same as alimony.

MARITAL PROPERTY   Accumulated income and property acquired by the spouses during the marriage, subject to equitable division by the court. States will vary on their precise definition of what is to be included in marital property, sometimes excepting property acquired by gift or inheritance. (See *community property* and *joint property*.)

MISTRIAL   A trial that is terminated prior to its completion, due to the occurrence of some fundamental error that would render the trial invalid. Following a mistrial, the case must be tried again from the beginning.

MOTION   A written or oral application to the court for some particular relief, such as temporary support, injunction, or attorney's fees.

NO-FAULT DIVORCE   A marriage-dissolution system whereby divorce is granted without the necessity of proving one of the parties guilty of marital misconduct.

ORDER   The court's ruling on a disputed issue requiring the parties to do certain things or setting forth their rights and responsibilities. The order is reduced to writing and may be signed by the judge and filed with the court by agreement, without necessity of a court hearing.

PARENS PATRIAE   A doctrine whereby the state will take jurisdiction over any minor children living within its borders. This doctrine is the basis upon which certain states will assume jurisdiction in child-custody disputes, even though a divorce action was decided or is pending in another state.

PERSONAL JURISDICTION   The power of the court to order a spouse to do a particular thing such as pay alimony or child support.

PETITION   A written application for particular relief from the court. In some jurisdictions complaint for divorce is entitled "petition for dissolution." Some jurisdictions require that petitions be sworn and that the petitioners state under oath that the allegations contained in the petition are true.

PLAINTIFF   The party who files the lawsuit. Same as petitioner.

PLEADING   Formal written application to the court for relief and the written response thereto. Pleadings include complaints, answers, petitions, responses, motions, and all counter-pleadings.

PRAYER   That portion of a pleading, usually at the end, which specifies the *relief* that is requested of the court.

PRIVILEGE   The right of a spouse to make admissions to an attorney, clergyman, or psychiatrist, which are not later admissible in evidence.

166

REBUTTAL The introduction of evidence at a trial that is in response to new matter raised by the defendant at an earlier stage of the trial.

RELIEF Whatever a party to a lawsuit asks the court to do: dissolve the marriage, award support, enforce a prior court order or decree, divide property, enjoin certain behavior, dismiss the complaint of the other party, etc.

RESPONSE The pleading filed in answer to the allegations of a petition. The response may also allege affirmative defenses to those allegations.

RULES OF EVIDENCE The rules that govern the method of presentation and admissibility of oral and documentary evidence at court hearings or depositions.

SEPARATE MAINTENANCE A cause of action for support in cases where the spouses live in separate households; same as legal separation.

SETOFF A debt or financial obligation of one spouse which is deducted by the court from the debt or financial obligation of the other spouse.

SETTLEMENT The agreed resolution of disputed issues.

SETTLEMENT AGREEMENT The settlement reduced to a written document.

SHOW CAUSE (Same as Rule to Show Cause) A contempt-of-court proceeding to enforce court orders, judgments or decrees which have been violated. The alleged violator is given an opportunity to show cause why he should not be held in contempt or to comply with the court order. Failing both of these, the court may find the violator in contempt of court and may enter sanctions in the form of fine or imprisonment. The latter is a last resort, where all other efforts at compliance with the court order have failed.

SPECIAL EQUITY A special interest in property arising from the agreement of the parties or due to some special contribution toward the acquisition or preservation of the property.

STATUS QUO The existing state of things; leaving things as they are without modification or alteration. "Things" can be anything from visitation arrangements to property rights.

STIPULATION An agreement between the parties or their counsel, usually relating to matters of procedure.

SUBPOENA A document served upon a person who is not a party to the action, requiring him to appear and give testimony at a deposition or court hearing. A subpoena is normally accompanied by a witness fee set by statute, as well as a mileage fee for transportation costs to and from the place to which the individual is subpoenaed. Failure to comply with the subpoena could result in punishment by the court.

SUMMONS A written notification to the defendant that an action has been commenced against him, and requiring that the defendant appear within a specified period of time to answer the complaint.

SURREBUTTAL Testimony offered by the defendant to counter any new matter contained in the rebuttal testimony offered by the plaintiff.

TEMPORARY MOTIONS Application to the court for interim relief pending the final decree of divorce, separate maintenance, or annulment. Typical temporary motions include motions for temporary alimony, child support, attorneys' fees, custody, visitation, enforcement or modification of prior temporary orders. The court enters a temporary order after hearing a temporary motion.

TESTIMONY Statements under oath by a witness in a court hearing or deposition.

167

TRIAL   A formal court hearing to decide disputed issues raised by the pleadings.

VACATED   When a court order, judgment or decree is somehow defective, it is vacated—that is, eliminated—and either a substitute order is entered or a new hearing is granted, which will ultimately result in a new order, judgment or decree.

WITHOUT PREJUDICE   Orders, judgments and decrees that are entered without prejudice can be modified at a later time without the necessity of proving a material change in circumstances justifying the modification. Orders are normally entered without prejudice by agreement rather than as a result of a court hearing.

BIBLIOGRAPHY

Divorce   (Specific Grounds, Examples, Psychological, Financial)

Coping: A Survival Manual for Women Alone. Martha Yates. Englewood Cliffs, N.J.: Prentice-Hall, 1976.

Creative Divorce: A New Opportunity for Personal Growth. Mel Krantzler. New York: M. Evans, 1974.

The Custody Handbook. Persia Woolley. New York: Summit Books, 1979.

The Custody Trap: Helping Children of Divorce. June and William Noble. New York: Hawthorn Books, 1975.

Dealing with Divorce. Robert K. Moffett and Jack F. Scherer. Boston, Mass.: Little, Brown, 1976.

Divorce and Decision-Making. Christina Robertson. Chicago, Ill.: Follett, 1979.

The Divorce Experience. Bernice and Morton Hunt. New York: McGraw-Hill, 1977.

Divorce: The Man's Complete Guide to Winning. Lauren O. Vail. New York: Sovereign Books, 1979.

Everything You Want to Know About Your Husband's Money . . . & Need to Know Before the Divorce. Shelley Aspaklaria and Gerson Geltner. New York: T. Y. Crowell, 1980.

The Fighter's Guide to Divorce. Robert Blackwell. Chicago, Ill.: Regnery, 1977.

Getting Custody: Winning the Last Battle of a Marital War. Robert H. Woody. New York: Macmillan, 1978.

How to Divorce Your Wife. Fordin Athearn. New York: Nordon Pubns., 1977.

How to Get Out of an Unhappy Marriage. Eugene Walder. New York: Putnam, 1978.

Marital Separation. Robert S. Weiss. New York: Basic Books, 1975.

No-Fault Divorce. Michael A. Wheeler. Boston, Mass.: Beacon Press, 1974.

The Trouble with Lawyers. Murray Teigh Bloom. New York: Simon & Schuster, 1969.

Uncoupling. Norman Sheresky and Marya Mannes. New York: Viking, 1972.

What Every Man Should Know About Divorce. Robert Cassidy. Washington, D.C.: New Republic Books, 1977.

169

Children and Divorce

The Boys & Girls Book About Divorce. Richard A. Gardner. New York: Bantam, 1971.

Talking About Divorce: A Dialogue Between Parent & Child. Earl A. Grollman. Boston, Mass.: Beacon Press, 1975.

What Every Child Would Like Parents to Know About Divorce. Lee Salk. New York: Harper & Row, 1978.

About the Author

JAMES T. FRIEDMAN is a specialist in family law. In addition to his private practice, he has, since 1970, been regularly engaged in drafting family law–related legislation on behalf of the Illinois State Bar Association, the Chicago Bar Association, and the American Academy of Matrimonial Lawyers. He has been a member of the Chicago Bar Association Legislative Committee since 1979, is a member of the American Academy of Matrimonial Lawyers, of the American Bar Association Family Law Section, and the Illinois State Bar Association's Family Law Council. He is the author, editor, and publisher of the *Illinois Family Law Report* and has written many articles for legal journals on divorce, child custody, and other related matters. Mr. Friedman lives in Illinois with his wife, Carolyn. The Friedmans have three children.